I0528659

OFF

de

CANNES FESTIVAL

(2003 – 2024)

ALAIN ZIRAH & ANNE GOMIS

Copyright © 2024 by Alain Zirah & Anne Gomis

Paperback: 978-1-960861-92-4
eBook: 978-1-960861-93-1
Library of Congress Control Number: 2023923181

All rights reserved. No part of this publication may be reproduced, distributed, or transmitted in any form or by any electronic or mechanical means, without the prior written permission of the publisher, except in the case of brief quotations embodied in critical reviews and certain other noncommercial uses permitted by copyright law.

This is a work of nonfiction.

SWEETSPIRE LITERATURE
— MANAGEMENT —

OFF
de
CANNES FESTIVAL

(2003 – 2024)

Books by the same author

Strass & Paillettes – Le journal d'un festivalier,

(AZ Productions, Marseille, 2011)

Dieu a créé la femme à son image,

(Éditions Thierry Sajat, Paris, 2014)

Du sang sur le tapis rouge – Kat Ladies,

(Prix Art Freedom 2016 - Éditions Thierry Sajat, Paris)

Rock Fictions (1976-2016),

(Société des Écrivains, Paris, 2017)

Dans les coulisses du festival de Cannes

(Société des Écrivains, Paris, 2017)

Interdit aux Hommes

(La Librairie Numérique de Monaco, 2018)

Cannes Backstage - Dans les coulisses du festival

(Nombre7, Paris, 2023)

Dieu a créé la femme à son image,

(Éditions Thierry Sajat, Paris, 2023)

God created Woman alike herself,

(Prime Seven Media, Tomah, Wisconsin, USA, 2023)

In this book, you will discover what the Cannes Film Festival really is, as Alain Zirah and Anne Gomis experiences it, every year, for eleven days, since its first festival in 1983. How do you get on the red carpet? How do we know where the best evenings are going and how do we get in? How do you get invited to jet-set parties and meet the world's greatest stars? Should we ask Brad Pitt or Steven Spielberg for an autograph, if we have the chance to meet them?

In parallel, we will discover how an idea was born in the author's mind to create his own event within the great Cannes event. The Cannes Film Festival has become the world's biggest event after the World Cup, more important, but only once every four years. We will be able to follow the veteran's journey and all the necessary human adventures to highlight new talents at events and evenings, including the famous evening ceremony.

Will Alain Zirah and Anne Gomis be able to organize their OFF DE CANNES festival events? We will also learn how to set up and prepare a film, short, medium or long, and here too we will have to overcome all the obstacles of the obstacle course.

Nothing predisposed the author to find himself at the very heart of the most advanced artistic creation. He was born in Marseille, in a city that has always favoured football over culture. He does not come from a family of artists known and recognized in the profession. On the contrary, he had to go through all the steps, with the force of his wrist. In a hostile environment. Today, he is part of the artistic avant-garde in the fields of cinema, fashion, writing, music and the visual arts. Because to want to make Total Art, it was first necessary to find the places, study the codes and customs of these different professions and immerse yourself in them like a chameleon. The place is not a city in France or elsewhere. It's the Cannes Film Festival. A unique place for only eleven days. And Alain Zirah gives you the rules, tips and tricks to become, in your turn, a must. Because, in Cannes, during the festival, everything is possible. That's what we're going to find out.

The Cannes Film Festival is governed by codes. They must be respected. First the dress code. Tuxedo for gala evenings and some parties. There's no way we're going to be invited to Chopard dinners or the Eden Roc without a bow tie. Casual attire, but classy, is still a must for other evenings. And of course, for white evenings, linen or cotton are welcome. The white tuxedo is recommended only if it is well worn. In most other cases, you will spend your time explaining that no, we're not the waiter. And that for champagne, it's better to go to the bar.

Alain Zirah and Anne Gomis discover talents in cinema, music, fashion, writing and fine arts with the Five Views organization, which organizes the Great International OFF DE CANNES Web Competition, every year in May, during the International Cannes Festival.

To be on the carpet, all the men are in tuxedo. For girls, two possible choices: either a long dress of a couturier or designer, tastefully cut in quality fabrics, with possibly a slit on one side to show a leg; or a dress or a short skirt on very high heels. Bustiers, shirts, tops and caracos are welcome. Strass and glitter are recommended. We are not at a job interview for a permanent position in the capital; we are in Cannes. We're in a good mood and we're here to celebrate. And to meet a lot of people.

Let the show begin...

INTRODUCTION

For its new spring, Cannes, the beautiful city, has put on its suit of light, a lark mirror in which everyone comes to dream of a Better World. Under a sunny azure, she walks her split dress from the Majestic to the Martinez before climbing the stairs under the crackling of the photographers. Cannes, center of the world, crossroads of humanity, celebrities, pomp and futility, Cannes, capital of dreams, is hosting its film and political festival. Multilingual cradle of a world of jetsetters where business is done in the evening, in sumptuous villas or on billionaire yachts. Here, even the photographers are in tuxedos. Cannes, the beautiful one, makes her Chopard jewelry shine in a French Palm Beach where the casino attracts fewer people than its terrace renamed VIP Room. Palms are less tall than their cousins in California, but at their feet, evening wear is out every night, and often also during the day. Hollywood is an unattainable dream, but American stars are ready to compromise for a simple golden palm. In his time, *Señor Presidente* Tarantino explained that after winning the gold medal for his film Pulp Fiction, being president of the jury was the highlight of his life. What distinction can bring more brilliance to such an honor? Perhaps the ascent of the steps on the famous red carpet, twenty years later, with Uma Thurman and John Travolta, in May 2014, for Olivier Assayas' film Sils Maria.

Cannes, the beautiful one, got up at noon, had lunch at the Farfala or *la Potinière du Palais* at four o'clock and only went to the luxurious garnet velvet salons of the Majestic to exchange a few words, a few business cards before going to change. It's going to be a long night. You will have to attend the screenings after having presented your best profile by walking the red carpet and not fail to honor all your friends. Above all, don't forget anyone! Photographers' flashes are a water of youth for women's skin. Such repeated flashes are like a facelift to erase the years. The light enters through the eyes of the pretty women and settles inside to make them shine. That's why they do their seduction act, with their high heels planted in the red carpet, their split dress proudly displaying the harmonious shape of a tanned or very pale leg, like an alabaster statue. Cannes spent hours getting her hair, make-up and clothes done. From now on, she is there to be desired; to be desired by the photographers who shout her first name, to be desired by the crowd of festivalgoers who circulate her name in the back rows. The photographer knows that his salary will depend on a beautiful portrait. The beautiful and uncertain anonymous, tired by the fatigue of having kept their place for two hours, despite the games of elbows, take over their idols.

"She is smaller than on TV!" 'She doesn't look so nice!' "I thought she was prettier!" 'She's even more beautiful than on TV!' "What a class! What an aura!"

The bodyguards left her the center of the red carpet so that she could shine with a thousand lights, alone like a diamond on her velvet case. We photographed, filmed, admired, applauded, coveted, then moved on to another, equally sparkling one. We practice zapping people. And the luckiest enter the dark rooms, holding the precious invitation against his heart. Precious sesame!

After the film, everyone tries to join the sumptuous parties in the most sumptuous villas in the heights of Cannes, California or on the road to Vallauris. It will be difficult to leave Villa Man Ray and its magnificent swimming pool above the sea to join the producer friends at Villa Babylone with its human foosball table. Champagne flows freely and the best caterers have competed to provide the most refined dishes and opulent buffets. The scallop lote is a delight for the palate; others will only swear by the calisson, verrines or the macaroon jars... There is something for everyone. The Carlton, the Majestic and the Martinez are the scene of a reunion.

In recent years, new places have come to seek public notoriety and recognition. This is how some prestigious establishments appeared, including the Gray d'Albion near the Majestic. The former Festival Palace will house the ceremonies since 1949. In 1988 it became the Noga Hilton and from 2008 to 2010, the Palais Stephanie before becoming the JW Marriott Hotel and since 2012 hosting the VIP Room which was previously located at Palm Beach. The festivalgoers came from all over the world and prepared, for months, their stay for these two weeks. Everyone meets and kisses each other with hugs and shouts. A call later, we find ourselves at the Noga Hilton or the Martinez singing with the pianist. We are all part of a big family, and we are happy to meet again, every year, for twelve days out of time. We hesitate between Playboy or Europacorp parties, so we go to both. Everyone dances on the beaches. But, anyway, we know we'll end the night at the Baron. On the ground floor of hotel 3.14. The evenings will be punctuated for ten years by DJ Greg Boust. It is better to avoid overly flashy or eccentric outfits if you don't have an invitation. If security asks you to wait a moment, it means you have a good head and you will be home in 30 to 60 minutes. If, on the other hand, the security says no, you're done. It is better to avoid any irritation. Anyone who wants to make a splash will only succeed in getting himself or herself permanently excluded from the parties. Because the physiognomics, at the entrance, recognize your face and they have memory.

OFF DE CANNES 2011 & JACKSON FAMILY

May 17, 2011

Following Alain's meetings with Simon Sahouri, President of the Jackson Family Foundation, and Marco Derhi, President of Clean and film producer, at the Petit Bar du Carlton in May 2010, and their meeting in Marseille a few weeks later, Alain Zirah and Anne Gomis are very proud to have been asked by the Jackson Family Foundation, and then mandated by **Joseph Walter Jackson**, patriarch of the first musical family, to organize the first visit of the Jackson family to Cannes. The father of the King of Pop, who died tragically on 2009, June 25, at the age of 50, was welcomed to Villa Oxygene by Richard Nilsson. He comes with Dieter Wiesner, Michael and Janet Jackson's manager, as well as Simon Sahouri and Marco Derhy. Joseph Jackson tells Alain that his "son was the greatest American dancer. There was Fred Astaire, Gene Kelly and Michael Jackson!" He is fascinated by Anne who, he says, resembles his aunt when she was young. Faced with her charm and dazzling smile, he accepts a kiss on the cheek. An extremely rare occurrence, we're told.

During the press conference, hosted by Richard Nilsson in Villa Oxygene, the Jackson Family Foundation launches the first Michael Jackson museum in the house where he was born, in Gary, Indiana. Popa Joe Jackson announces signing of contract to launch a theme park called Happy Land, in Ho Chi Minh City, Vietnam with a 2 billion dollars budget.

For the Matrix Reloaded film, a bubble was built on the port to accommodate 800 happy fews to promote the sequel to the cult film with a budget of one million dollars. Alain Zirah and Adrienne McQueen are greeted by **Keanu Reeves** and Hugo Weaving. photo : Alain Zirah

Senegalese-born rapper **Akon** raises $ 1 billion to fund projects on the African continent and electrify millions of homes with solar power. Alain Zirah and Didier Moulion congratulate him on his 2016 Heart Fund charity gala at the Carlton.

« Meeting **Francis Ford Coppola** is an exceptional moment. Of course, The Godfather and Apocalypse Now are cult masterpieces that will go down in cinema history. For twenty minutes we talk about music, comics and his life routine.

Francis reveals his passion for Grateful Dead, the Beatles and Richard Wagner. About comics, he knows and appreciates the work of French cartoonist Moebius. On the other hand, he directed Dracula but never heard of Philippe Druillet, whom I introduced him to. Then we join Gerard Depardieu and Carole Bouquet for a cocktail party in honor of the film CQ (2001) directed by his son Romain Coppola. »

« If you come to Zoetrope studios I'll be happy to see you again. »

Photos : Alain Zirah

« Spending an evening at Al Charq, the best Lebanese restaurant in Cannes, also means the pleasure of convivial dinners. American actor **Bill Murray** is delighted to rub shoulders with Princess Adji Biagi. "Alain, write me a script and we can shoot a film in Guinea Bissau, in Anne's country with her family. But after that, I'm not sure I want to go back to the States. »

Since 1983, it's been all about cinema, directors, actors and actresses. In 2003, we came up with the idea of giving our friends and family the benefit of our contacts with the world of music and all art forms. Anne Gomis' special relationship with **Youssou N'Dour**, who has known her since she was 18, or with **Keziah Jones** and his musicians, has taken the Cannes OFF to every continent. A good way to build bridges with Anne Marie d'Estienne d'Orves' Five Continents Jazz Festival of Marseilles.

Spending time with **John Waters**, author of Female Trouble and Polyester, in palaces is as joyful as attending the filming of MR 73 with actor **Daniel Auteuil** and meeting him on a sailboat party for his film Marius, based on Marcel Pagnol. I love my life, I work and I enjoy it.

OFF DE CANNES

THE ORIGINS

Once again, this year, during the Cannes Film Festival, only the magic of cinema counts. Hundreds of events take place at the same time. Cannes is so dense; everyone comes to find what they have come to look for. It is the Tower of Babel of dream and fantasy.

For a few days, the whole of humanity lost interest in current events in the world. There can be wars in the world, famine, misery or the biggest football game, nobody cares. We have militated before, we have denounced in films or articles, but now we no longer think about it. For a moment, we only live for the cinema, for Cannes and for its festival.

If the Cannes International Film Festival is the biggest event in the world, within this festival, the Cannes OFFs are a unique event. It was created in 2005 by Alain Zirah, join by Anne Gomis since 2011, organized with an organization and mostly with a lot of good will. A regular at Cannes since 1983, Alain Zirah has noticed that all the great directors have started with short films. Today, New Talents express themselves with digital cameras, smartphones and broadcast their videos on the Internet. The purpose of the Cannes OFFs is to discover, highlight and support the New Talents of the 21st century, present in Cannes during the festival. The Cannes Film Festival serves as a sounding board to promote these artists suddenly drawn from the shadows. Let's start at the beginning.

Alain Zirah & Anne Gomis

Alain Zirah & Solene climb the red carpet to open the Cannes festival, highlighting their characters AZ & Ladykat. Below: with British screenwriter Peter Ramsey and composer Michael Errington, then screenwriter Germaine Kos and American actor Clement von Frankenstein.

2005 - THE ORIGINS

Cannes - May 2005

- I beg your attention, please?!

The multilingual clientele of the Majestic turns their faces towards the young stranger in a tuxedo, Cannes is the center of the world, every year for twelve days, in May. People come from all over the world, fascinated by rhinestones and sequins, standing, stiletto heels stuck in the red carpet under the magic flashes of the lenses. The looks question.

- Who is it? Who is it?
- Your attention, please!!!!!

The enchanted words are released. The unknown also speaks English. Many American producers look inquisitive under the sunglasses of their sunglasses.

- Let me introduce you to a very talented artist.

Alain Zirah explained that the goal was to introduce multi-talents artist, and not only speaking about movies, actor, actresses and film makers. After a few minutes, the directors applauded, immediately accompanied by the actresses with exuberant lipsticks. The concept is popular. Alain Zirah presents a talented young American artist. The director of photography on some big productions has just started making short films. He plays the guitar, launches into a new style of dress and keeps his first blog Rocket Pictures, baby, in which he tells about his own Cannes festival daily. The shock partner Ladykat pins a plastic brooch covered in gold paint. Young director **Mark W. Gray** has just received the first "Palme d'Or OFF de Cannes" for his blog on the Cannes Film Festival. This is the first time a blog has been awarded during the Cannes Film Festival. A cult evening!!!!!
The bet is won! The operation was successful.

"During an evening at Villa Man Ray, in 2005 May, I had won a haircut offered by one of the great hairdressers of Antibes street. I choose red hair without suspecting that, in an after -party, on the Beach, the director Jim Jarmusch would introduce me to the sumptuous **Selma Hayek**. I spent a delicious evening with her, speaking English and French. I didn't want to risk speaking Spanish. She introduced me to the Serbian director Emir Kusturica. I couldn't imagine that he will become the first OFF de Cannes patron, in 2007. At the beginning of our conversation, Emir Kusturica didn't spoke to much. He just wanted to understand who we are and what we expected from him. The director, born in Sarajevo, won The Palme d'Or twice for *When Father Was Away on Business* and *Underground*. He asked to think.

So, with Jim Jarmusch and Fatih Akin, we talked about David Bowie and Selma introduced me Javier Bardem and Sam Shepard. Then I talked again with the sumptuous actress and after long conversation we finished to pose for a picture. The beautiful Mexican actress appreciated the picture and used it to sell her Isabel brand jewelry. We had no news from Emir Kusturica..."

The evening after the official *Star Wars Party*, AZ & Ladykat, within a chronicle entitled *"Glitter & Glam"*, awarded two OFF de Cannes golden palms under the supervision of the director **Emir Kusturica** for the 60th Cannes Film Festival. And were welcome to a Carlton Beach party by **Guillermo del Toro**.

The ceremony to award the OFF de Cannes Golden Palm was to be an event on the scale of this prestigious anniversary with partnership of Hewlett Packard, Fiction TV and White Lotus Club. With a representation of several countries gathered for the occasion in the lounge of the Martinez Hotel, Emir Kusturica sponsored the presentation of the OFF Golden Palm to **Hugo Mayer** for his spectacular blog on the 2007 Cannes Film Festival: Le Blogreporter.

A second golden award was specially set up to highlight the work of **Farid DMS Debah**, director/producer for his short film "*The Executioner of the Innocents*". This work is more commendable as Farid has just acquired, with his brother Yassine, a recording studio in Normandy and as he is embarking on the production and direction of his first feature film for the cinema.

From the Majestic lounge, the Lou Reed photographer from London, Robert Leslie, helped the young team to immediately send an article to inform the medias of the event. The first article about OFF de Cannes was written by Monia Kashmire.

ALAIN DELON & JANE FONDA
AT OFF DE CANNES

May 2007

The 2007 OFF de Cannes took place in the lounge of the Martinez hotel, in front of the entrance of the restaurant *La Palme d'or*. The golden letters shine above the several countries gathered for the 60th Cannes Film Festival. Attending this new event are a young Georgian director, two young Russian actresses, a Togolese woman and a Sikh Indian actor and director, Surendra Singh. The Serbian director Emir Kusturica was seduced by the concept and agreed to be the patron to award two OFF de' Cannes golden palms. Alain Delon and Jane Fonda come to support the event. The Samurai waved his thumb while my son Pierre, 15 years old, was thrilled to see "The star of L'Oreal". Indeed, if he has never heard of Alain Delon, he has noticed the many posters showing Jane Fonda, muse of the brand partner of the Cannes Film Festival. It will take years for me to introduce him to *Borsalino* and *Barbarella*. **Hugo Mayer** expresses himself with a not feigned emotion:

> To my great surprise, AZ & Ladykat, Hewlett Packard, Fiction TV and the White Lotus Club awarded me the gold medal for the 2007 Best Blog of the Cannes Film Festival! LadyKat herself pinned the OFF de Cannes Golden Palm on my tuxedo, in the living room, in front of the entrance of the Martinez Golden Palm restaurant, under the amused eyes of Emir Kusturica, who congratulated me! I'm very moved, I didn't expect it at all. As a gift, I received the magnificent book *"Le Festival de Cannes"* seen by Emanuele Scorcelletti, where I am shot behind Brad Pitt and Jennifer Aniston, in 2006...
> Thank you, friends!

The young director **Farid DMS Debah** is also awarded a palm awarded by Emir Kusturica for his short film *The executioner of the innocents*. After directing an eleven-minute short film entitled *Art'n Acte Production*, he began directing and producing his first feature film for the cinema.

> We are fortunate to have with us two journalists, Monia Kashmir and her colleague write the article immediately. The article is immediately sent to the AFP agency thanks to the connection of the photographer Robert Leslie who shows us the photos of Brad Pitt that he has just taken and must send to his agency. For the first time, the OFF de Cannes are being covered by the media.

PORTRAIT

Photos Fox Eye.

Créative, observatrice, exigeante, elle travaille avec minutie et transmet à la pellicule la générosité, la sensibilité et l'humanisme qui l'habitent. Elle, c'est Brigitte, photographe qui se fait appeler de son nom d'artiste : Fox Eye. Portrait.

FOX'EYE, DANS LES YEUX DU « GUÉPARD »

Autodidacte, Brigitte se décrit comme une « passionnée d'images, sans cesse à la recherche du mouvement pour figer l'instant, capter les émotions, les sensibilités, donner de la matière, du relief, de l'impact, toujours à la recherche de l'imperceptible pour ne jamais lasser le regard ». Car avant toute chose, l'œil·eye cherche à capter les émotions et les sensibilités, donner de la matière, du relief et de l'impact pour ne jamais lasser le regard. À Cannes où nous l'avons rencontrée, elle venait tout juste de remporter le Grand Prix international de la photographie OFF de Cannes 2019. La photographe des stars y était récompensée pour la qualité de ses photos artistiques mais également pour sa personnalité attachante, son grand cœur et sa disponibilité. Un instant magique qu'elle n'oubliera pas de si tôt. « C'était comme un rêve de petite fille enfin réalisé. Je n'étais jamais venue ici auparavant pendant le Festival. Croiser tous ces acteurs c'est tellement incroyable pour moi ». Pourtant, des stars Fox Eye en a croisé même si l'une d'entre elles l'a sans doute marquées plus que les autres. « Je me souviens de la première fois où j'ai rencontré Alain Delon. Brigitte était alors secrétaire du maire Jean-Claude Gaudin. Pour la première du film « Fabio Montale », elle était au service presse à préparer les badges et les accès VIP quand d'un coup Alain Delon surgit. » Il m'a glissé à l'oreille qu'il avait très envie de boire une coupe de champagne et qu'il ne le faisait jamais sans la compagnie d'une jolie femme. J'ai bu cette coupe de champagne dans le bleu de ses yeux ».

C'était en 2002 se souvient Brigitte. Elle la revoit au Festival de Cannes cette année. Le monstre sacré y était invité pour y recevoir une palme d'honneur. « J'étais au Carlton et on m'a dit d'Alain Delon allait arriver quand il est passé. J'étais à 50 cm de lui. J'ai pu encore une fois croiser son regard et le photographier à bout portant » se souvient-elle des étoiles encore plein les yeux ».

ODV

PASSIONNÉE D'IMAGES, SANS CESSE À LA RECHERCHE DU MOUVEMENT POUR FIGER L'INSTANT, CAPTER LES ÉMOTIONS, LES SENSIBILITÉS, DONNER DE LA MATIÈRE, DU RELIEF, DE L'IMPACT

ZIK ANIMATION PRÉSENTE

FRATER'CITÉ 4 — 16 juin 2019

L'ÉVÉNEMENT QUI NOUS RASSEMBLE

75, CHEMIN DE FONTAINIEU · MARSEILLE 14ème
AVEC PRÈS DE 40 ASSOCIATIONS ET PARTENAIRES MARSEILLAIS

www.marseille-plus.fr   27

Alain Delon is an animal. French cinema's most emblematic actor is expected in the Palais du Festival, where he is to receive an honorary Palme d'Or for lifetime achievement. We're parked in front of the Bar des Célébrités. Our godfather, Paul-Loup Sulitzer, is seated, given his age and health, and tells us that he hosted the actor in his early days. An electric hum. The hurried man strides like a panther, his gaze fixed. He's focused, and says to the audience: « It's a bit of a posthumous tribute, but it's for my lifetime. »

AZ & Ladykat shot some short films during 2005 Cannes festival compiled in a DVD under the title *Ladykat seek the quest*. During the exhibition of AZ's painting in Galerie l'Eclat de Verre (2007) with the Kat Ladies' catwalk shot for the series screened in La Ciotat Best of festival and the Kat Ladies Party in Marseilles Red Lion (2009) before Cannes festival.

I have met **Tim Burton** several times with whom we talked about memories of his town of Burbank. He really liked the Kat Ladies characters. Catwoman revisited with Michele Pfeiffer was a visual shock. We met again in Annecy, in a much less heated atmosphere, during which I shot a portrait of Alice in Wonderland' s director in a flowerbed.

- "The Kat Ladies, what is it exactly?"

Quentin Tarantino was very attentive when I presented him with my first DVD with a short entitled *Ladykat seek the quest* in the Majestic. He kept getting excited. Wow, it's great! Then, I met him several time and gave him a DVD when he was with his producer Harvey Weinstein.

During another of our conversations, we were at the Carlton Bar. He was very receptive. I explained how much how much I love the quality of his films and place references to the greats of cinema in my first series entitled *Les Femmes chats*. He really appreciates it. I am a young amateur filmmaker, and I'm shooting footage with a camcorder for episodes in disorder. We're in the age of MySpace and Dailymotion, where episodes are posted as they're edited, with no regard for the linearity of the story. The words of Quentin Tarantino are there to encourage me. In everything, there must be a beginning. I make the mistake of not asking him, and when we leave, he says I'll watch your film. So, don't hesitate to ask what you need when you have a unique opportunity. Our last meeting was in 2019, in Carlton Bar. We organize our event in the same place. I invite him, but his planning to promote Once upon the Time... in Hollywood is too tight. Next time...

THE INTERNATIONAL CANNES FILM FESTIVAL

There are few places on the planet that have not heard of the Cannes Film Festival. Probably a few tribesmen attached to worshipping the forest' spirit rather than those strange Westerners resembling penguins worshipping Brad Pitt and Penelope Cruz. Since its creation on September 20, 1946, the Cannes Film Festival has made the world dream. Many professionals and enthusiasts fly more than ten hours by plane to come to the Croisette. Everyone will hope to leave with what they came for. All the people will leave with memories full of memories, business cards and photos. Some will come to spend a weekend or a few days there. The aficionados will stay for the eleven days and will block the dates of the next festival on their agenda one year in advance. But the objectives are not always the same. See the maximum number of films from the different selections. See and photograph stars. To meet professionals. Be noticed in the hope of finding a casting director who will introduce you to the very closed world of film shoots. Shooting a film or looking for people who could help finance it. To be invited to the most private parties. See or meet the most beautiful girls on the planet. Meet friends in one of the restaurants, on the beach, or in one of the palaces. To look pretty to meet a billionaire. Make selfies. But always this incessant dream: to shine. Alone or accompanied by a star in a photo now intended for social networks. The stars range from Michèle Morgan and Brigitte Bardot to Nicole Kidman and Scarlett Johansson, from Jean Cocteau and Alain Delon to Quentin Tarantino, Angelina Jolie and Brad Pitt, from Sophia Loren and Anthony Queen to Jim Jarmusch and Penelope Cruz... So many names that already call for dreams. And of course, we dream of being able to climb the red carpet one evening.

The walk up the Cannes red carpet is the most popular and eagerly awaited event on the Croisette. Everyone has their own methods for obtaining tickets, the precious sesame for the screening. Some movies are in great demand, others are more accessible, especially those by distant directors and unknown actors. There are several staircases, but the most important is the 7 p.m. one, with compulsory tuxedos for the men and evening gowns for the ladies. These are the times when stars are monopolized by product placement agencies who lend them dresses and jewelry.

We are ready with my faithful friend **Patrick Lachaud**, Caroline Gregeois, Cassandra Gava, Nathalie de Monaco and Franck Katz

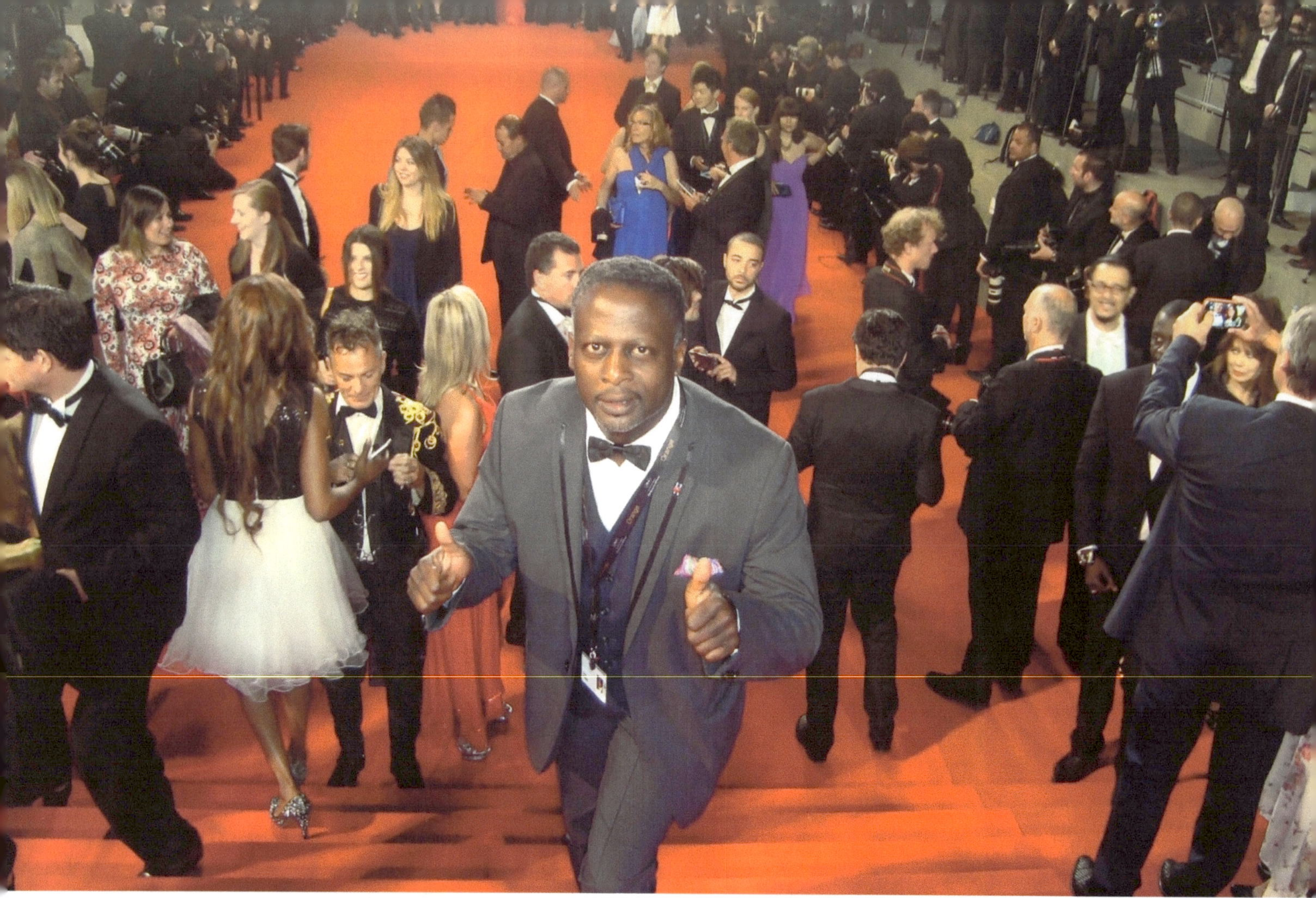

Every year, the Cannes Film Festival takes place in May. Often from the second week of May. The sun is often shining, and it is an opportunity for some to take the first sea baths of the year. Other years are less fortunate, and Leonardo DiCaprio must open the festival with an umbrella to present the film Gatsby the Magnificent.

In 2001, the Cannes Film Festival was directed by President Gilles Jacob, Executive Director Veronique Cayla and Artistic Delegate Thierry Fremeaux, who oversaw the film selection. In 2007, he became General Delegate to Gilles Jacob, who remained President until his retirement. After 38 years of running the festival, Gilles Jacob became Honorary President in 2015. The former CEO of Canal+, Pierre Lescure, becomes President of the Cannes Film Festival on January 14, 2014. They are the ones who, each year, will select the films that will be in the official selection of the Festival (films in and out of competition).

Several sections have been created over the years: *Un certain Regard, Cinéfondation, la Quinzaine, la semaine de la Critique*. Over time, the duration of the festival is reduced from fifteen days to eleven days.

Since 1983 or 1984, the Cannes Film Festival has been held in the Palais des Festivals et des Congres, 10,000 m2 by the sea, nicknamed the bunker.

The Cannes Film Market, with 12,000 participants, is the first in the world with approximately €620 million in contracts signed in 2019.

With an annual budget of 23 million euros by 2022, and over 3,000 jobs, the Cannes Film Festival brings together over 40,000 accredited professionals from 160 countries and nearly 5,000 journalists and technicians for over 2,000 media outlets every year. The city's population triples from 75,000 to over 200,000. Spin-offs from the event amounted to 196,840,600 euros in 2017. This figure is expected to rise to over 200 million by 2022.

The red-carpet measures 60 meters, on the 24 steps of the Festival Palace and along the floor. The 2022 festival used 2160 meters of red carpet, as it is changed three times a day for 12 days. The 36 screening rooms welcome over 80,000 guests.

360,000 flutes of champagne were consumed during the 2023 edition with 15,000 bottles of champagne uncorked in 12 days at the Majestic and 3,000 cigars consumed at the Martinez...

The Festival screens nearly 80 films in different sections.

Official selection:

Feature film competition: some twenty feature films by regular filmmakers at the festival compete for the Golden Palm every year.
Out-of-competition: high-budget feature films are presented in galas but also in special sessions (opening or closing of the festival, midnight sessions...).

Un Certain Regard, created in 1978, offers about twenty films, including experimental marginal films, from both great filmmakers and beginners, on the fringes of distribution. The jury awards the Un Certain Regard and related prizes.

Short films: films less than 15 minutes long are screened there for the Palme d'or for the short film.

Cinefondation: created by Gilles Jacob in 1998, supports fiction films of less than one hour in length, coming from different film schools around the world, assisted in production thanks to the foundation's workshop. With the possibility of having a residence in Paris, assistance with scriptwriting and screenings in Parisian cinemas.

Cannes Classics: since 2004, has been showing classic films by cult filmmakers. Free screenings are held with the beach cinema.

Parallel sections:

Critics' Week: created in 1962 by the French Syndicate of film critics, selects only first and second films by filmmakers from around the world. And, since 1988, a selection of about ten short films. The best film receives the Grand Prize.

The Directors' Fortnight: created in 1969, it selects about twenty feature films and ten short films. The jury awards the Camera d'or and rewards the work of a director with the *Carosse d'Or*.

ACID programming: created in 1993 by the Association of independent film makers for distribution, often includes works by young filmmakers who do not have distributors.

CINQ REGARDS (2003-2024)

Originally, Alain Zirah used to come every year to the Cannes International Film Festival, the Annecy International Animation Film Festival and the Avignon Festival, whose OFF brought an explosion of artistic and cultural activities. At Cannes, everyone was talking about cinema, directors, actors and actresses. The idea was to put the spotlight on singers and musicians, writers, stylists and models, and painters. With the advent of digital cameras, the first bloggers arrived in Cannes in 2005. The Festival refused to accredit them. "You're not journalists, you're not photographers, and you're certainly not filmmakers! Alain decided to welcome them and show them off. This was to be the start of the Cannes Festival OFF awards. These were soon to become the OFF de Cannes.

"It'll never work!"

The mayor of Cannes, Bernard Brochand, summons Alain and Anne: "Who are you? What do you want? You're overshadowing the Cannes Festival!"
-"But there are only two of us!"

When the couple explain their objective, the mayor congratulates the initiative and supports the author, who has just published the book *"Glitter & Glam"*, by sitting next to her on the live program *Midi en France* on France 3, presented by **Laurent Boyer** and Frédéric Soulié. The adventure takes off again in 2018 with the support of Gilles Jacob, former General Delegate and then President of the Cannes Film Festival. All good things come to those who wait.

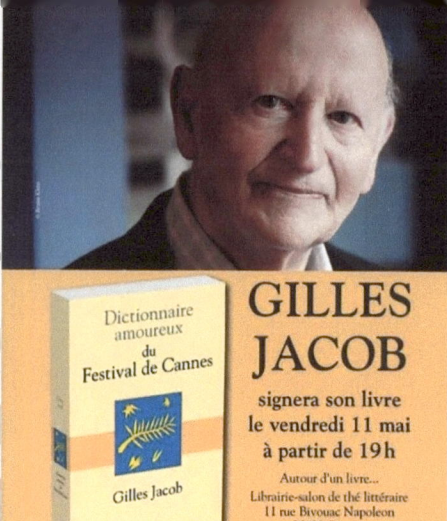

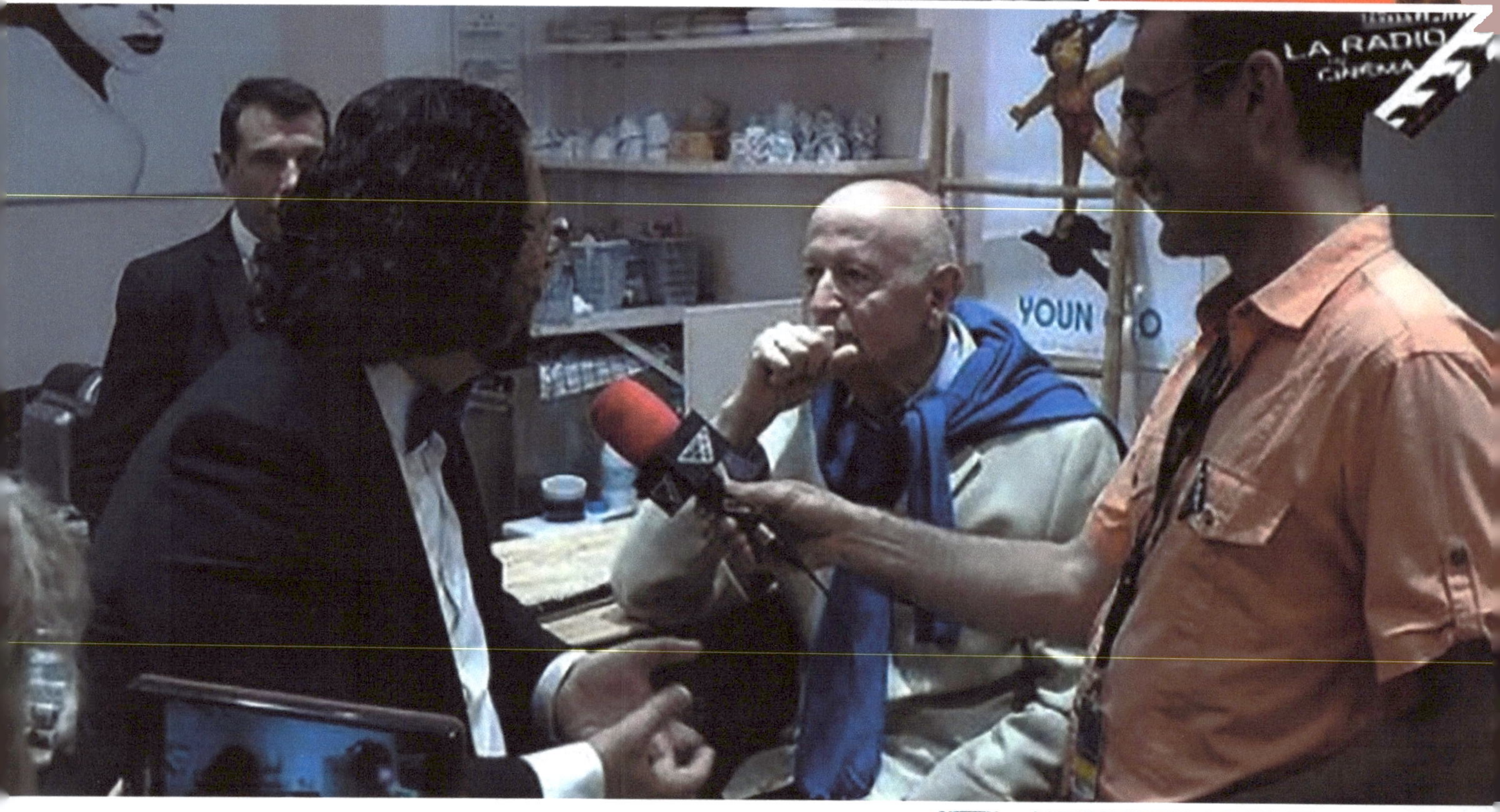

GILLES JACOB

signera son livre
le vendredi 11 mai
à partir de 19h

Autour d'un livre...
Librairie-salon de thé littéraire
11 rue Bivouac Napoleon
06400 Cannes

PLON
www.plon.fr

Alain ZIRAH
Le fondateur des
OFF de Cannes
signera son livre
le dimanche 13 mai
à partir de 16h

Autour d'un livre...
Librairie-salon de thé littéraire
11 rue Bivouac Napoleon
06400 Cannes

On Friday 2018, May 11 and Sunday May 13, the tea-room called *Autour D'un Livre* located opposite the Palais du Festival, brought together three authors specializing in the festival. *Le Dictionnaire Amoureux du Festival de Cannes* evoked **Gilles Jacob**'s 40 years as festival director, and Alain Zirah recounted his behind-the-scenes anecdotes. After the book signing and presentation by Anne Gomis, Gilles Jacob answers Alain Zirah's questions in a cross-interview with Radio de Cannes journalist Patrice Caillet. Finally, the Cannes Film Festival supports the OFF de Cannes.

OFF DE CANNES 2023

WHAT IS IT EXACTLY?

The year 2023 is a very rich one, with a succession of events including a presence at Paris Fashion Week in the Westin Paris Vendôme palace in March. This was followed by a day at Skyfall on May 20, with a panel discussion on ecology, the launch of the *Cannes Backstage* book, the creation of a live painting, international fashion shows and showcases for singers and opera singers. Les OFF de Cannes are partners of the Superstar Gala organized on May 22 by May Liu's Superstar-Art-Foundation, with fashion shows around the swimming pool of a villa in Le Cannet with **Beauty Queen Corazon Ulgade Yellen**. An appearance at Monaco's Hôtel Hermitage to support Tiffany McCall's fashion shows.

After introducing the franco-thai designer Parisa at their two Cannes events, the OFF de Cannes help her to organize a party at Crystal Paris on June 18. Editions Thierry Sajat reissues Alain Zirah's book *Dieu a créé la Femme à son Image*, which is immediately published by American publisher Prime Seven Media under the title *God created Woman alike herself*. New event at the Westin Paris Vendôme, on October 1, for AEFW Paris Fashion Week and Creativ Magazine (New York). Participation in the Hero Festival, then in book fairs and other Literary meetings.

Queen Corazon Yellen Ulgade, Beauty Queen & celebrity – Enoka Fonseka

ALAIN ZIRAH & ANNE GOMIS

AI helps us to Produce Fashion Shows

As OFF DE CANNES festival's French producers, Alain ZIRAH and Anne GOMIS, made several events during 2023 to help their 9,000 artists to get international visibility. You can learn in the updated Wikipedia presentation, translated in several languages, how the OFF DE CANNES festival highlights the artists. Alain ZIRAH went for years to the International Cannes Film Festival. All the festival goers only spoke about movies, actors, actresses and directors. In 2005, he decided to create a new festival inside the festival. The goal was to bring to all kinds of Arts. Now, the artists express themselves in cinema, music, dance, fashion, literature, photo/video, fine arts, visual arts, bloggers and influencers, and now AI for 2024…
https://fr.wikipedia.org/wiki/Off_de_Cannes

Now, OFF DE CANNES festival also became an actor involved in the fight for the Climate and the preservation of Biodiversity. With Didier POULOS and Herve LECHEVALIER, they organized a roundtable of specialists in ecology with Zachary James MILLER for the OBAMA Foundation in 2023, May 20 in the Skyfall Cannes.

Alain ZIRAH was very involved in his role as jury for the 2022 Manila International Fashion Film Competition founded by John Guarnes and Bench Bello. With Anne GOMIS, they made the audience's eyes shine during 2023 Fashion catwalks in Cannes, Paris, Marseilles, Monaco...

The Fashion Shows highlighted several designers as Angela SHAPOVALOVA, Eptissem GASMI, Chic Image (Skyfall, Cannes), Parisa for Risa Stone, July of St Barth (Le Crystal, Paris), Miss Jasmine and Princess Gloria for Samoa Somao (Pool Party in Marseilles). They make Enoka FONSEKA grow from the Cannes Festival to the magnificent ballroom of AEFW for the Fashion Week in Westin (Paris Vendôme). They support their partner Tiffany McCALL (Hotel Hermitage, Monaco) with the presence of Patriarch Abrahamic Hereditary and at Hotel Bristol, Paris. It was the right place to dedicate his books.

Singers have been in the spotlight all year long, lyrical voices with the baritones Richard Rittelman and Michael Guedj and the incredible voice of the soprano Lidia Izossimova. The aim was also to showcase the rising generation of young artists as the singers Maelys Luna, Mariastella Sardi, Lina from Boheme Production which were in the famous French The Voice Kids 2023, but also the young model Jenaya Lee and the models of the school bring by their English teacher Magali Lombrana aka Maglala (Lila, Lina, Clara, Naïs, Aida, Emilie, Alexia, Caroline, Sasha, Fabio…)

Published in 2023, Cannes Backstage (Nombre7) is a biography of the sparkling couple and tells 40 years of the Cannes festival. It has just been translated into English for 2024 by Prime Seven Media which also published God created Woman like Herself for USA & UK meanwhile Thierry SAJAT editions made it for France.

To celebrate his career as writer, Alain ZIRAH received an Awards from Lithe-Litho (a medieval city of le Castellet, in the South of France). As multi talented artist, Alain showed some of his Visual Arts on the Superstar Museum, a metaverse platform created by May LIU, from Dallas, USA, and received a Superstar Awards for best NFT during the Superstar Gala at Cannes festival, on May 22.

Since they were mandated by Joseph JACKSON, patriarch of the first musical family, to organize the first venue at Cannes of the Jackson Family Foundation, in 2011, Alain ZIRAH and Anne GOMIS want to associate Artists, Entrepreneurs, Scientists and committed Citizens to turn waste into clean energy for Africa, first. They use the resonance chamber of international artists to bring to light the values of ecology and ecological transition. "We'll continue Michael JACKSON Tribute's Heal the world to extend the partnership we began in 2011".

So, if you are an artist and want to prove you are a "talent of tomorrow", become a OFF DE CANNES member on https://www.helloasso.com/associations/cinq-regards/adhesions/adhesion-membres-des-off-de-cannes.

If you are a creative cinema, music, dance, fashion, literature, photo/video, fine arts, visual arts, bloggers and influencers, and now AI for 2024…You can already send your photos, videos, music, etc. through the 2024 GREAT INTERNATIONAL WEB COMPETITION for international visibility with the 19th edition on the platform https://www.facebook.com/internationalwebconcours

---

The OFF de Cannes are present at Paris Fashion Week in the Westin Paris Vendôme palace, in March and october 2023 and Alain received a SUPERSTAR Awards for Best NFT from May Liu, Dallas, USA (article in GANAP Magazine, Manila, Philippines, and INTEGRITY Magazine, London, UK).

ALAIN ZIRAH FROM FRANCE TO STATES

Alain Zirah is one of the few French authors published in the USA. He surprised his colleagues in Marseille at the 2nd la Ciotat book fair, on September 24, by presenting his new book God created Woman alike Herself. Published by Prime Seven Media from Tomah, Wisconsin, near Chicago, his collection of poems and philosophical tales will be distributed in English-speaking countries (USA, Canada, Australia, India, China, South Korea...). Released in 2014, the French version was republished in an updated and expanded edition by Thierry Sajat, in June 2023, for France and French-speaking countries.

This book will help convey the French art of living and promote women's rights internationally. Maybe it could open the door to the populations of Iran, China and some African countries which consider women as inferior. These publications complement the Prize Lithe Litho awarded to Alain Zirah in recognition of his body of literary work from the medieval village of Le Castellet. The trophy was awarded in 2022, December at the Continental-Hôtel Dieu by Catherine Merveilleux, editor-in-chief of Marseille magazine.

Alain Zirah was back in Paris on October 1st, for Fashion Week at the Palace Westin Paris Vendôme, where he came to support the fashion designer Enoka Fonseca, awarded by 2018 OFF DE CANNES Grand Prize de la Mode and Coup de Coeur 2021, now highlighted by Rex Christy Fernando and presented by Tony Para. He reunites with Princess Esther Kamatari from Burundi, the first black model for Paco Rabanne, who was godmother of the OFF DE CANNES in 2012. Alain dedicates to her his book tribute to women, at the Hôtel Bristol, near the Palais de l'Elysee. The following day, at the Cafe de Paris on the Champs Elysees, he dedicated his book to Debora Denecke, a famous international makeup artist, who want to open up the Brazilian market to him.

Another string to his bow, Alain Zirah is also a digital artist. A selection of his digital works highlighted in the Superstar Museum, a museum in the Metaverse, were presented in Dallas and then New York (Rockefeller center) for the whole world to see. Created by American producer May Liu, the Foundation presented him with a Superstar Award during the Cannes Film Festival in May 2023, along with a Japanese team. One of his works ended up on the Museum's main page. He has also been named Ambassador and jury member for the next Superstar Gala, to be held in Las Vegas on November 19. On the same date, his American book will be presented at the Miami Book Fair. That's America

MIAMI BOOK Fair

Immerse yourself in a world of words at the extraordinary Book Fair, where stories come alive and imaginations soar.

November 18-19, 2023

Wolfson Campus of Miami Dade College in Downtown Miami

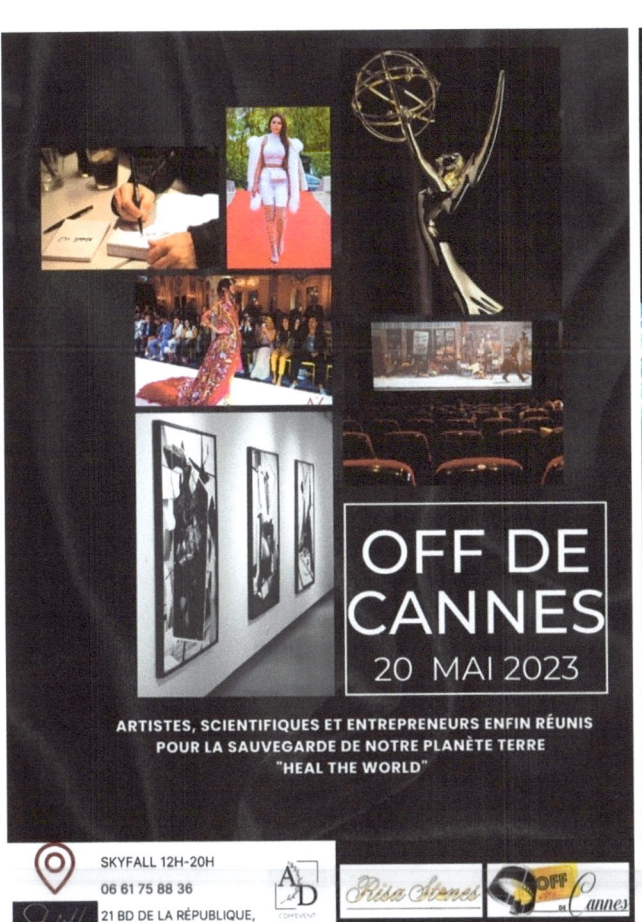

OFF DE CANNES
20 MAI 2023

ARTISTES, SCIENTIFIQUES ET ENTREPRENEURS ENFIN RÉUNIS POUR LA SAUVEGARDE DE NOTRE PLANÈTE TERRE "HEAL THE WORLD"

SKYFALL 12H-20H
06 61 75 88 36
21 BD DE LA RÉPUBLIQUE, CANNES

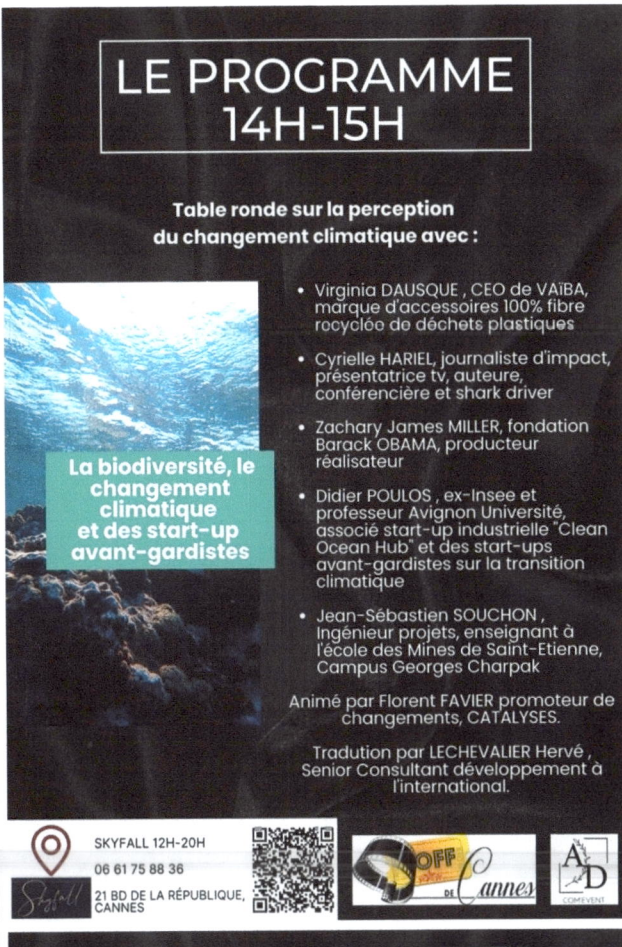

LE PROGRAMME 14H-15H

Table ronde sur la perception du changement climatique avec :

La biodiversité, le changement climatique et des start-up avant-gardistes

- Virginia DAUSQUE , CEO de VAÏBA, marque d'accessoires 100% fibre recyclée de déchets plastiques
- Cyrielle HARIEL, journaliste d'impact, présentatrice tv, auteure, conférencière et shark driver
- Zachary James MILLER, fondation Barack OBAMA, producteur réalisateur
- Didier POULOS , ex-Insee et professeur Avignon Université, associé start-up industrielle "Clean Ocean Hub" et des start-ups avant-gardistes sur la transition climatique
- Jean-Sébastien SOUCHON , Ingénieur projets, enseignant à l'école des Mines de Saint-Etienne, Campus Georges Charpak

Animé par Florent FAVIER promoteur de changements, CATALYSES.

Tradution par LECHEVALIER Hervé , Senior Consultant développement à l'international.

SKYFALL 12H-20H
06 61 75 88 36
21 BD DE LA RÉPUBLIQUE, CANNES

LE PROGRAMME 15H-19H

CHANTEURS

CAROLE DE LYS - FRANCINE CAZANOBE
CHRISTINA GARCIA - DOINA CIOBOTAR
RICHARD RITTELMANN - RYAN MANSOUR - THELMA - SATY DJELASS (GIMS FAMILY)

FASHION SHOW BY T.L BEAUTY CENTER

ANGELA SHAPOVALOVA (2G FASHION)
CHARLENE ASSONI (CHIC IMAGE)
EPTISSEM GASMI - PARISA (RISA STONES)
ENOKA FONSEKA

ARTISTE PEINTRE

JULES RENARD (LIVE PAINTING) - PHILIPPE VALY - MARIE FRANCE, LAETITIA ET MARTINE BASTELICA

PERFORMERS

SAXOPHONISTE PATEUF (BB PROD) - LAETITIA AYMES - GRAINETTE (BOMBE À FLEURS) - LITA CY
MISTER ÉLÉGANCE - DJ DIRTY FINGERZ + ROZTEA BEATZ

DÉDICACE DE LIVRES

"CANNES BACKSTAGE" BY ALAIN ZIRAH
JEAN-FRANÇOIS CIRANNA

START-UPS INNOVANTES

GRAINETTE - VAÏBA - CLEAN OCEAN HUB

SKYFALL 12H-20H
06 61 75 88 36
21 BD DE LA RÉPUBLIQUE, CANNES

OFF DE CANNES ET L'ÉCOLOGIE

EN 2023, LES "OFF DE CANNES" ÉLARGISSENT LEURS AMBITIONS AVEC L'OBJECTIF DE SENSIBILISER AUX VALEURS DE L'ÉCOLOGIE, LA PRÉSERVATION DE LA BIODIVERSITÉ ET DE LA TRANSITION ÉCOLOGIQUE EN ASSOCIANT ÉTROITEMENT ARTISTES, ENTREPRENEURS, SCIENTIFIQUES ET CITOYENS ENGAGÉS.

REVUE DE PRESSE

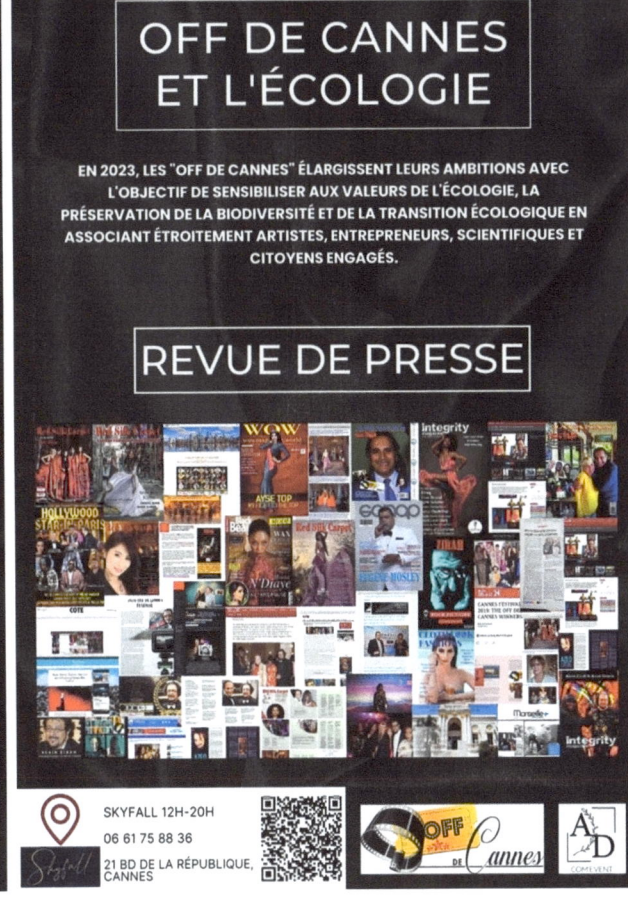

SKYFALL 12H-20H
06 61 75 88 36
21 BD DE LA RÉPUBLIQUE, CANNES

CANNES 2023

Mister Jojo Photography

MMORTALISER UN INSTANT DE VIE

The Festival screens nearly 80 films in different sections.

Official selection:

Feature film competition: some twenty feature films by regular filmmakers at the festival compete for the Golden Palm every year.
Out-of-competition: high-budget feature films are presented in galas but also in special sessions (opening or closing of the festival, midnight sessions...).

Un Certain Regard, created in 1978, offers about twenty films, including experimental marginal films, from both great filmmakers and beginners, on the fringes of distribution. The jury awards the Un Certain Regard and related prizes.

Short films: films less than 15 minutes long are screened there for the Palme d'or for the short film.

Cinefondation: created by Gilles Jacob in 1998, supports fiction films of less than one hour in length, coming from different film schools around the world, assisted in production thanks to the foundation's workshop. With the possibility of having a residence in Paris, assistance with scriptwriting and screenings in Parisian cinemas.

Cannes Classics: since 2004, has been showing classic films by cult filmmakers. Free screenings are held with the beach cinema.

Parallel sections:

Critics' Week: created in 1962 by the French Syndicate of film critics, selects only first and second films by filmmakers from around the world. And, since 1988, a selection of about ten short films. The best film receives the Grand Prize.

The Directors' Fortnight: created in 1969, it selects about twenty feature films and ten short films. The jury awards the Camera d'or and rewards the work of a director with the *Carosse d'Or*.

ACID programming: created in 1993 by the Association of independent film makers for distribution, often includes works by young filmmakers who do not have distributors.

OFF DE CANNES AND ECOLOGY - MASTERCLASS ON BIODIVERSITY

On 2023, May 20, the OFF DE CANNES are expanding their ambitions with the aim of raising awareness of the values of ecology, the preservation of Biodiversity and the ecological Transition, by closely associating Artists, Entrepreneurs, Scientists and committed Citizens.

Organized by Didier Poulos and Herve Lechevalier, the American Zachary James Miller, representing the Obama Foundation, which trains tomorrow's young leaders, explains at a round table what the USA is doing to heal the planet.

CANNES BACKSTAGE
Dans les coulisses du festival

Alain Zirah

Le festival de Cannes raconté par le fondateur des OFF de Cannes.

Comment se passe vraiment le plus grand festival du monde ? Comment avoir une vie de rêve pendant dix jours ? Comment fait-on pour monter sur le tapis rouge ? Comment côtoyer les plus grandes stars internationales dans les palaces et les soirées privées ?

Artiste amateur ou professionnel, découvrez tous les conseils et les anecdotes qui vous permettront de gagner du temps et, comme l'auteur, de côtoyer stars internationales et professionnels du cinéma, de la musique, de la mode. Producteurs, distributeurs et médias seront à votre portée.

Alain Zirah est un artiste multi-talents, tour à tour photographe, écrivain, réalisateur et artiste-peintre hypnotique. En 2005, il crée les OFF de Cannes. Avec le Grand Concours International du Web, Alain Zirah et Anne Gomissont sont devenus des ambassadeurs de la culture française à l'international. Dans les recueils Rock Fictions, Dieu a créé la Femme à son image suivi du livre Interdit aux Hommes et dans ses films, l'auteur apporte une vision très originale et documentée sur le monde actuel. Il a reçu de nombreux prix, dont le WOW Awards de Best Artist 2020 (Londres) et le Prix Lithé-Litho 2022 pour l'ensemble de son œuvre littéraire avant d'exposer ses peintures hypnotiques à New York.

NomBre7 éditions

CANNES BACKSTAGE
Dans les coulisses du festival

Alain Zirah

23€TTC

ISBN 978-2-38351-646-0

CANNES BACKSTAGE
Dans les coulisses du festival
Alain Zirah

NB7

CANNES BACKSTAGE
Dans les coulisses du festival

Alain Zirah

Essai

For the release of his book Cannes Backstage, Alain Zirah gives several presentations of the biography devoted to the two OFF DE CANNES co-producers, Alain Zirah and Anne Gomis, as well as 40 years of the Cannes Festival. It's also time to sign dedicaces at Skyfall club and the Carlton, as well as during the Superstar Gala organized by Chinese-American director **May Liu** with **Alan Landry** and **Parisa**. A way to talk of the true about some of our close international stars.

OFF DE CANNES 2022

In a period still shaken by the consequences of the Covid-related health crisis, and after some hesitation as to whether the Cannes Festival would finally be held in May 2022, the OFF de Cannes team is moving towards a musical showcase project enhanced by a Fashion Show, with several international runway shows.

THE FASHION ART SHOW CASE PROJECT

10h – 13h BRUNCH MUSIC ART

Exhibitions of paintings, sculptures and photos in a sumptuous villa. Presentation of NFT and digital Art. Writers' autographs. Opening with avant-garde artists and music lounge with catering stands, world cuisine, beverages (champagne, wine, cognac) - French art of living.

14h – 19h FASHION SHOW CASE

Non-stop fashion show by international designers + showroom mixed with musical showcase + lyrical artists with huge possibilities to be validated together. Dance show, performers, comedians with show hypnotist.

20h BEFORE SHOW OFF DE CANNES

Reception of jury members, VIPs and personalities...

Trophies awarded to writers and visual artists, designers and models, dance and show performers. Fashion show by the winning designer. Showcase for the 3 artists in the music category pre-selected and presented by the jury, with public vote, followed by presentation of the trophy to the winner.

22h OFF DE CANNES NIGHT

Headliner show. Official photo of all participants with artists and headliners.

23h – 2h DJ MIX SHOW

Prestige Party DJ – danceurs – performers - champagne.

THE AFRICAN UNION'S CULTURE AND ECONOMIC DEVELOPMENT PROGRAM AT THE CANNES FESTIVAL 2022

LE CONSUL GÉNÉRAL DU SENEGAL

The President Macky Sall, Senegal has taken over the presidency of the African Union on February 5, 2022. The Consul General of Senegal has therefore asked the OFF de Cannes team to organize a cultural program to enable the African Union and European Union delegations to make connections.

The Cinq Regards team supports this project and values the investment, foresight and awareness of these two organizations, in which Africa has a major role to play. The OFF de Cannes are proud to participate, in all humility, in the implementation of this initiative which is close to their hearts. So, for this project, on May 20, 2022, Senegal will present Africa, its tourism, economy and ecology, meetings rich in discoveries as well as strategic and cultural development perspectives. Artists and cultural works (cinema, fashion, plastic arts, music, dance, gastronomy, literature) will be in the spotlight. The goal is also to communicate the values of Europa and Africa in Asia with the partnership of GANAP TV International (Manila, Philippines).

The presence of the presidencies of the African Union and the European Union at the Cannes Festival will highlight the tourism, cultural and entrepreneurial potential of the countries of these two continents. Alain Zirah and Anne Gomis, who have been organizing events in Cannes for 17 years, have been commissioned to organize this year's event.

The aim is to involve artists from the worlds of cinema, music, dance, fashion, writing, the visual arts and the culinary arts in raising public awareness of ecological values.

The work of Ababacar Diene, in charge of Culture at the General Consulate of Senegal in Marseille, also helped to highlight the young singer **Talima C.,** a finalist in the Voice Kids 2019 mentored by coach Pascal Obispo, whom the OFF de Cannes are keen to spotlight on an international level.

9000 ARTISTS FOR 2 BILLION PEOPLE INHABITANTS OF THE AFRICAN-EUROPEAN CONTINENT

The objective was ambitious: "We were approached by the Consulate General of Marseille on behalf of the Republic of Senegal, President of the African Union, for one year. This 75th festival was a unique opportunity to bring together the African Union and the European Union, via Presidents Macky Sall (Senegal) and Emmanuel Macron (France), to send a message of peace to 2 billion people, benefiting from the resonance of the Cannes festival."

The idea was for the Senegalese delegation, accompanied by Senegalese beauties in traditional dress, to climb the steps around international star Omar Sy on May 18, to surround the Senegalese star with a speech after the film Les Tirailleurs, produced by the actor, to announce the establishment of a day to pay tribute to the Tirailleurs from different communities "drawn from elsewhere" to save France.

Then a celebration in the gardens of the Villa Rothschild, bringing together representatives of Senegal and the French government, the mayors of Cannes and Marseille and other consuls, to announce the establishment of cooperation agreements at a press conference before the musical showcase and fashion show, featuring several fashion shows by leading African and European designers, which drew rapturous applause from 1,500 guests.

In partnership with Filmfestivals.com, 50 American directors and producers were on hand to offer advice and support to African professionals. Specialists in industrial engineering and health were ready to announce actions to combat hypertension and diabetes.

The pool of 9,000 artists from the Cannes OFF were ready to bring valuable cultural, ecological, economic, tourist, health and social messages to the attention of the two continents. The public will more readily accept instructions in favor of ecology from artists, where politicians are not necessarily heard.

To everyone's surprise, the two governments cancelled this unique opportunity. Senegal cancelled the event just as Ivory Coast was gathering a host of celebrities around Sharon Stone to present a trophy to Madame Dominique Ouattara. Parliamentary elections in France and the Dakar International fair prevented representatives from both continents from addressing the world's population via the 5,000 international journalists present in Cannes for the 75th anniversary. It will be difficult to postpone the event, as the Czech Republic will take over the presidency of the European Union on July 1, 2022.

« Let's hope together that we can implement this project in the future, so that future generations can eat fish without plastic micro-particles. To convey a message of peace in Ukraine and other countries around the world. »

ALAIN ZIRAH & ANNE GOMIS
SENEGAL AT THE CANNES FESTIVAL

After more than 15 years dedicated to artists, Alain Zirah and Anne Gomis take a new impulse. For their 17th edition, the OFF de Cannes festival put this year their spotlight on a country: Senegal. Very invested in its missions of opening to the West, thanks to President Macky Sall, Senegal has obtained the presidency of the African Union for one year, from February 15, 2022. The OFF de Cannes would like to support all his investments, his clairvoyance, his awareness in this world in which Africa has a major role to play. The Secretary General of the UN, António Guterres, said that the success of the UN in the world rests on its success in Africa. The OFF de Cannes will be proud at their modest level to participate in this initiative which is close to their hearts and to let the greatest number know the importance of the relations to be developed between Europe and Africa in the current geopolitical context (tourism, economy, ecology and of course culture).

Senegal will therefore present in Cannes, during the 75th festival, its tourism, economy and ecology at the service of international culture. Meetings rich in discoveries as well as in strategic and cultural development perspectives are planned. The institutions as well as the artists of Senegal, but also of various countries of the U.A. will highlight the wealth of their works (cinema, fashion, plastic arts, music, dance, gastronomy and literature) to present them to all the countries and lead them on the red carpet.

www.ganapmagazine.com

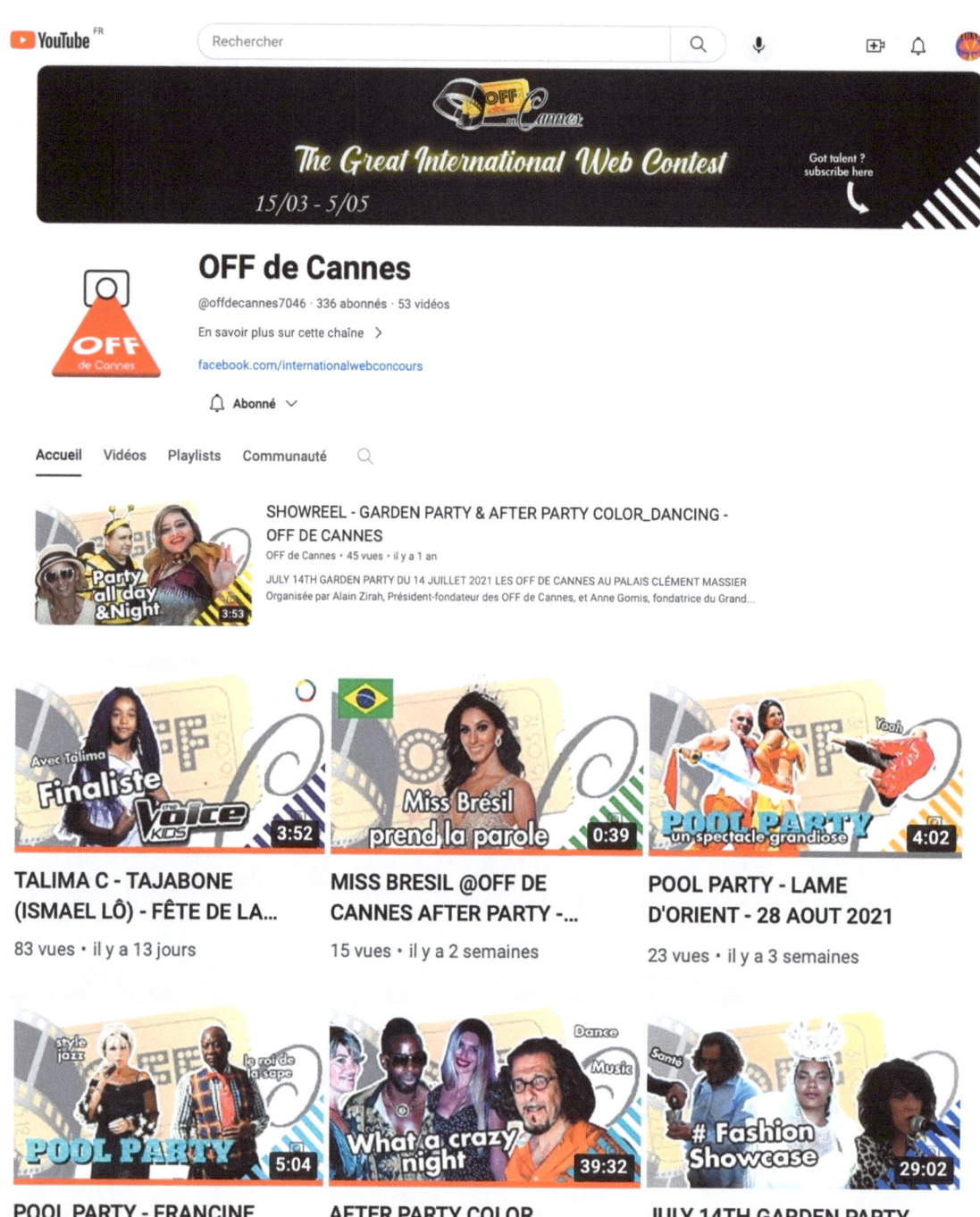

With the help of Myrthe Ekuba Bosenju and William Pereira, the OFF de Cannes team has set up a YouTube channel dedicated specifically to the OFF de Cannes and the Great International Web Contest. William took particular care in creating the channel's logo, thumbnails and miniatures to showcase the artists involved in recent events. Some fifty videos will be rolled out over the course of the 2022 edition.

Eliot Cohen, founder of Red Bus Studios Recording, in London, is the patron for that new adventure with Annie Kinnen, Patrick Lachaud and **Zachary James Miller**, representative of former president **Barack Obama** Foundation which trains young international leaders

AWARD-WINNING "THE KING'S CANE" ON RADISSON BLU ROOFTOP

Assisted by Myrthe Ekuba Bosendju, Florence Elomo, producer and Bambi Traoré, Ambassador representing the Consulate General of Senegal, Alain Zirah and Anne Gomis shed light on the first African blockbuster by **Reilinght Tchobo** and **François Kodjossiadan**, executive producer..

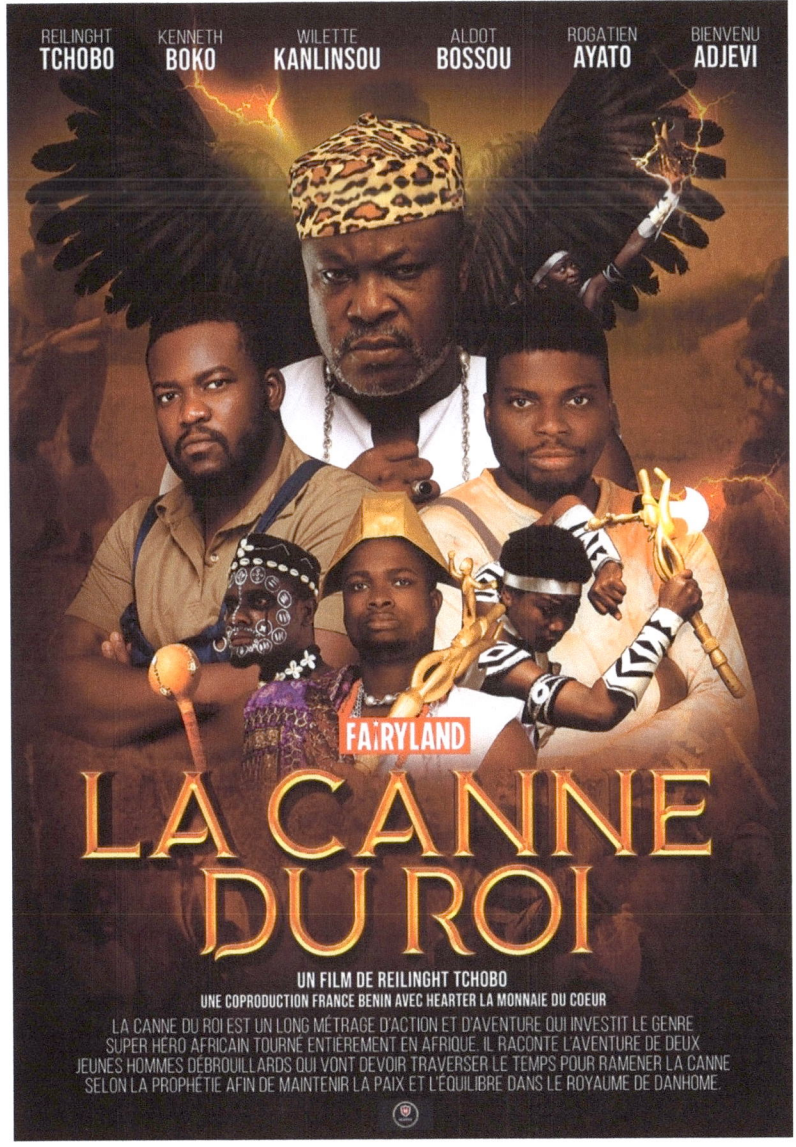

Gone, then, are the music and fashion shows scheduled for May 20 in the sumptuous private villa. The spotlight will be on Benin. On May 25, the ceremony took place in glorious sunshine, with hundreds of guests enjoying an exceptional panoramic view of the Bay of Cannes at Clara Gaye and Didier Moulion's RAF Production event, where cocktails were welcome. The OFF de Cannes Grand Prize for Movies was awarded to the movie The King's cane that was screened in theaters across Benin from July 1.

75TH CANNES FESTIVAL
ALAIN ZIRAH & ANNE GOMIS

Spazio Demo:
Alain Zirah you and **Anne Gomis** are known by our reader as **OFF de Cannes** producer. You both participate as jury members for Spazio Demo Future Models in march. We had the pleasure to meet you, Alain, during Cannes festival with Ayse Top, whom organized the models contest. How was your festival?

Alain Zirah:
The 75th Cannes festival was incredible. Anne Gomis and myself are very proudly and thankful to Stefano Piavani, your editor, with the charismatic Ayse Top, to introduce us to the competition and inside your magazine. The pleasure of meeting you in **villa Oxygene** was shared and, as I often say, pleasure is double when it is shared. Since several tears, social

networks change our way of life. We talk with Ayse Top since two years and had a cover of WOW Magazine together. But it was the first time we spoke in the real world with Ayse and I could hug Miss Netherlands Universe 2018 in my arms. This year was peculiar. Anne and myself were choose by the TV broadcast to represent **BBLACK AFRICA** during the festival.
So, Anne decided to organize from her desk with the back office team and I was very happy making the interviews in different places with cameramen.

Anne Gomis:
Cannes festival is the most important event for movies in the world. Since 2011, we're very happy to bring fashion shows, musicians, writers, singers and fine art artists in addition of the official film festival with our

Great International Competition. I must admit things became much difficult since the pandemic two years ago. For 15 years, with the **OFF de Cannes**, we have been helping artists moving from the local to the international level.
Last year, we were surprised to have many African artists from the Democratic Republic of Congo who participate to our contest. So, this year, for our 17th edition, we were approach by the Republic of Senegal, who received the presidency of African Union, after Congo, for one year. As a result, the 2022 OFF de Cannes direct their spotlights on the entire Africa. For its artists, but also for all its specificities. Originally from Guinea-Bissau, I was born in Dakar, Senegal, which makes me very proud to help my country. I feel so much patriot.

Spazio Demo:
Alain Zirah and Anne Gomis we knew you as ambassadors of French culture and lifestyle. We discover that your role is not only limited to the French culture to the attention of the different countries. Do you have a more political role?
Alain Zirah:
When I founded OFF de Cannes, in 2005, the first artists and bloggers that I chose to reward was American Mark W. Gray and then Farid DMS Debah, from Algeria, in 2007. The Serbian film director, producer and musician, Emir Kusturica, who won the Cannes film festival Palme d'Or twice, accepted to become the patron of our event organized in the Martinez lounge with a group of professionals from different countries. With the surprise visit of Alain Delon and Jane Fonda. We always been internationally oriented with the vocation to cross between them the various cultures.
We understood, this year, is the unique occasion to help African Union and European Union by presidents Macky Sall (Senegal) and Emmanuel Macron (France), to join forces to send a message of peace to 2 billion people. To stop the war in Ukrain, but also in

OFF DE CANNES 2021

THE GARDEN PARTY OF JULY, 14TH
FOR THE 15TH OFF DE CANNES ANNIVERSARY

Presentation of the Garden Party in GANAP magazine (Philippines)

The fashion designer Enoka Fonseka from Sri Lanka and her models

74TH CANNES FESTIVAL 2021

Organized to celebrate the 15th OFF de Cannes anniversary, the July 14 Garden Party highlighted the exemplary work of Anne Gomis, founder of the Great International Web Contest, which has since brought together over 9,000 artists. Together with Alain Zirah, these two producers bring international visibility to talents from the film, writing, visual arts, music and fashion industries. To bring them from the local to the international level. By the way, the OFF de Cannes are finally on Wikipedia. A guarantee of seriousness and respectability.

From noon, this musical festival brought a bubble of authenticity with the explosion of colors of Brazilian dancers setting fire to the Palais Clement Massier (Ladies Glam United and then Lame d'Orient), the presence on the stage of female artists evoking Saint-Germain-des-Prés (Adelia Martins, then Francine Cazanobe), the flights of the Saori-Jo keyboard

then Julianne (InFuzzion) allowed a demonstration of tap dance of the Swiss champion Angelo Borer (Crazy Feet) before the electro breakthrough (DJ Galaxy Cat).

The women were still in the spotlight with a fashion show composed of catwalks by a dozen designers supervised by Paulette Mouquet. Thus followed the creations from Abidjan (Emeline K) or Togo (Kombate Sylvanak), swimwear Amira Beautyful for Pretty Creation and bridal lingerie Ready Lady.

The swimsuits of Amira Beautyful for Pretty Creation.

The designer Asta Jakubson and her models in Jeanne of Arc's spirit

The Irish designer Asta Jakubson made a big impression by presenting, in exclusivity, her silver wire dresses, inspired by Joan of Arc. Designers and models were invited by all medias to pose for the event. The Sri Lankan stylist Enoka Fonseka received the OFF de Cannes Coup de Coeur Prize 2021 for her red dresses topped with flower crowns, also red. Women invaded the stage around the singer and guitarist Jean Marie Monteiro (Guinea-Bissau) then Bebert the hornet, the darling lent by Cyril Hanouna came to sing dressed as a bee.

Bebert the hornet joined by many women on stage

The male artists also made their voices heard with the lyrical flights of baritone Richard Rittermann in excerpts from operas including *Carmen* and *Turandot* by Puccini. A wonderful voice!

Immediately joined by the Indian artist Raghunath Manet, one of the masters of the vina, the latter also offered a sacred dance from Pondicherry, the former French trading post from which were originated *the Bayaderes*.

The visual and sound designer Devy Man presented his latest compositions accompanied by the dances of Shigemi Sawa, who came directly from Japan, in traditional dress. Alain Zirah and Anne Gomis joined Bruno Chatelin, president of the international jury of the OFF de Cannes and founder of the Filmfestivals.com platform, to present the singer Riker Lynch.

Indylov came to bring love to the audience and gave way to the Old School guitar of Will Barber, the singer selected by Zazie in the season six of the French show *The Voice.* The writer Lionel Gnali then received the PACA Films Prize of the Cannes OFF for the book adaptable to cinema, from the former minister Roland Dumas for his book *A broken destiny.*

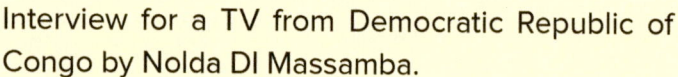

Interview for a TV from Democratic Republic of Congo by Nolda DI Massamba.

It was also time for the photo shooting with models by photographers as Tomasz Koperski and the interviews of the artists.

The event was followed live by four radios for Cannes, Marseille, Paris and Belgium. It was the right time in front of the cake of the pastry shop Sana Herbert the audience celebrate the 15th OFF de Cannes anniversary for the launching of the After-Party Color Dancing. It began with the hypnotic show by Olivier Gomis aka Magnetic which put to sleep one of the volunteers for a spectacular show. The party continued with the singer Malekoumsa, Saty Djellas, the presence of the sublime Miss Brazil, Barbara Vittorelli, with the unavoidable Stavroulla Nicolaou from Prestige Show Production, before a succession of DJ clubbing and a lot of people on the dancefloor....

Because of the pandemic, half a dozen members of the jury couldn't come to France. The team was so sad of a bad connexion so they were not allowed to talk on Zoom to some of the jury members as Bench Bello & John Guarnes (Philippines), Anuschka van Andel (Netherland), Motalib Bellouk (Marroco), Deborah Jay Kelly (England), Jean Pierre Beulaygue (France). No matter. The ceremony is postponed to a later date, in September. All the organization and guests were so sorry. So, they will be happy to listen the songs of Maria Pangilinan (Japan) with the other jury members Stavroulla Nicolaou (Cyprus), Max Ricciardi (France), Michael Lopes Cardozo (Netherland), Ayse Top (Netherland), Angelo Borer (Swizzerland), Rachanaa jain (England), Asta Jakubson (Ireland), Aleah Leigh (England) and Corazon Ulgade Armenta (United States). The two presidents of the international jury Bruno Chatelin (France) and Olympia A. Gellini (USA) and the president of European jury Richard Guedj (France) will annonce the winners of the competition with the godfather Eliot Cohen (England).

Three days later, Julia Ducourneau received the Golden Palm from the Cannes Film Festival for her second movie *Titanium*. The president of the jury Spike Lee, provocative and committed, is certainly at the origin of this supreme prize that rewards the young director. The second victory offered to a female director, in 74 years. Next year will be the 75th Cannes Film Festival. But many will wait for the announcement of the events planned for the 2022 OFF de Cannes. But next event in September for the OFF de Cannes ceremony on Zoom, for the first time

The opening of the After Party was the right time in front of the special cake made by the pastry shop Sana Herbert to celebrate the 15th OFF de Cannes special anniversary with the members of the jury.

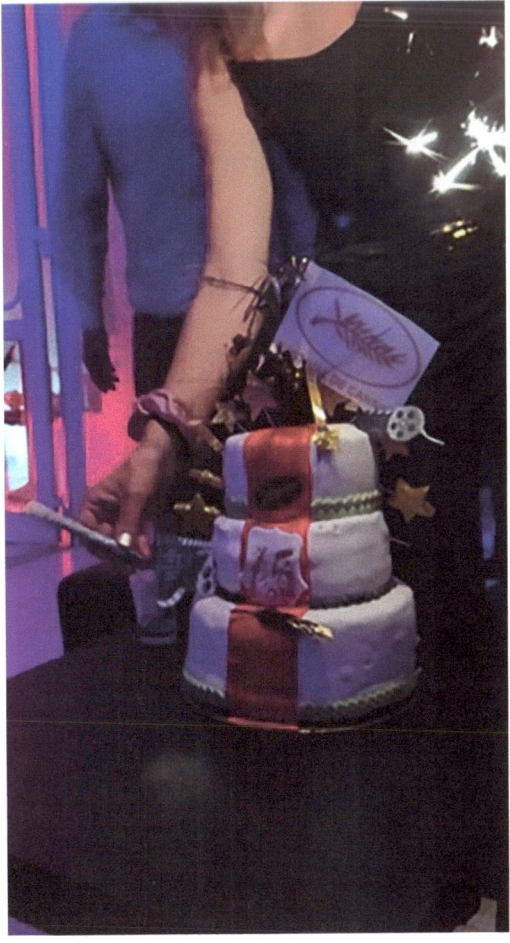

GARDEN PARTY OFF DE CANNES JULY 14ᵀᴴ, 2021

LONDON | PARIS | NEW YORK | LOS ANGELES | DUBAI | TOKYO | MANILA | HONG KONG

HOLLYWOOD

Special Cannes 2021

STAR IN PARIS

JULY 14, 2021 ISSUE

THE MAGAZINES

ELLIOT COHEN
RED BUS STUDIOS

ANNE GOMIS & ALAIN ZIRAH
PRODUCERS

JAZZ CORREIA

SISIKA

PAUL KABESA

MOH GREEN

LAURENT BILLIONAIRE

OFF DE CANNES CEREMONY AT PALAIS MASSIER
GARDEN PARTY JULY 14TH 2021
COPRODUCTION WITH RIVERA FIRST EVENTS & YAELLE PRESS

The multi-talented artist Paulette Mouquet, stylist and founder of the Ready Lady brand and head of several magazines, was a partner with a very important role to play in the Garden Party as artistic director of the international designers and models. She devoted an entire magazine to the OFF DE CANNES and the July 14 Garden Party, presenting all the members of the international jury.

Eliot Cohen & Red Bus Recording Studios, London, being presented with the prestigious Blue Plaque Award.

Eliot M. Cohen

Eliot founded the Red Bus Group of Companies in the 70s when he created and promoted the Hollywood Music Festival featuring such bands as Black Sabbath, Grateful Dead, Free, Traffic, Ginger Baker's Airforce and launching Mungo Jerry. Leslie Grade joined the board soon after which led to a close working relationship with the entire Grade family and Pye Records/ATV.

Over the past years Eliot has won several Ivor Novello awards, numerous gold discs, a BMI and ASCAP awards and gained a solid reputation in music publishing with International hits from Mungo Jerry, Imagination, Shaggy, Kelly Marie, Destiny's Child, Bananarama, Brian Johnson (AC/DC), Oliver Cheatham, Jocelyn Brown and Mariah Carey to name just a few. For many years, Red Bus Recording Studios, has provided facilities to record hits for a variety of international acts including George Michael, Spandau Ballet, Culture Club, Boy George, Alison Moyet, Brian Wilson (Beach Boys), Duran Duran, Tina Turner, Indochine, Richard Anthony, Robin Gibb (of the Bee Gees).

Culminating in Sony Music Publishing awarding Eliot Cohen with a very special record for 25 years of hit. In the 90s he created OVC Media to develop DVD and TV/Film production, and a DVD label. A documentary about Eliot's 35 years in the music industry was aired on Channel 4.

THE STARS OF
THE CANNES FILM FESTIVAL

Entering the Eden Roc parties organized by De Grisogono at Hotel du Cap is the certainty of meeting celebrities. May 22, 2006, the rapper **50Cent** has just taken a picture with Paris Hilton and before leaving, they kiss each other languidly. Curtis Jackson is delighted to show me his diamond ring, a symbol of success. We are talking about my son Pierre and the festival. Not only his movie or his *Candy Shop* title. Before leaving, we take the souvenir photo. But there's no way you're kissing me like Paris Hilton. It makes us laugh a lot.

On another date, 2009, May 21, the designer Christian Audigier announces the presence of Michael Jackson, Prince, Lenny Kravitz and 50Cent to celebrate his 51 birthday at the VIP Room in the Palm Beach of Cannes. Neither Michael Jackson nor Prince showed up, but the Kravitz and 50Cent show was a success in front of a packed place full of beautiful people, for one of the best parties organized by Jean Roch.

Opposite page: photo shooting on the beach AZ & **Ladykat** shot by Diane Von Schoen for *la Gazette de Saint Tropez*.

The great Germano-American actress **Diane Kruger**, 30, was married to Guillaume Canet when I first met her. She had shone in her performance in Helen of Troy, opposite Brad Pitt, in the film *Troy* which I had seen during the 2004 Cannes Film Festival. Between two *Benjamin Gates* films with

Nicolas Cage, we had good times with the director Fatih Akin, during parties on the beach.

I was very happy to see her win the Awards for Best Actress at the 2017 Cannes Film Festival for her role in the film *In the Fade* by **Fatih Akin**. No matter how notorious, you should never be surprised by the staggering slowness to put together a project and see it through to completion.

For my first film project, I had signed with Grenade Production for an animation with full 3D called *A Better world, in 2004*. It was a story about a crazy Adam and an astounding Eva in Eden's garden. I was very happy to propose to one of the best women in the world to join our casting. She was interested by the concept, *but my schedule is extremely busy*, she tells me. Being next to **Adriana Karambeu** made me beautiful. What is exceptional about the Cannes Film Festival is the possibility to approach the most beautiful women in the world.

In Cannes, anything is possible!

The project didn't go through, but it was delicious each time to talk with the beautiful Adriana. We met again in Paris and Marseille. What's incredible with her, each day, the photographers display all the previous day's photos for fans who want to treat themselves. In all the photos, Adriana captures the light incredibly well. She's exceptionally beautiful.

Cassandra Gava is very famous for playing the witch with wolves in John Milius' film Conan the Barbarian with Arnold Schwarzenegger. She told me how the scene lasted four days. She remained very close to him and actively participated in his political activities as Governor of California. We have known each other for a very long time and I had the pleasure of meeting her in Los Angeles, in 2003, where she produces action films.

At the end of the 2005 festival, we organized a picnic at the pool of Martinez. This Filipino woman is a strong personality and I consider her a loyal friend… It's always a pleasure to keep in touch and we walked up the stairs on the red carpet for a movie in 2015. What was funny, we were a team and get the first seats, two rows in front of the director and his actors. But the film was terribly trying. Very hard and violent. We didn't want to offend the director, but we couldn't bear the ordeal. Discreetly, our entire team left the theater, happy to be back in the holiday mood on the beaches of the Croisette.

After seeing his 2006 film *Pan's Labyrinth*, we were accompanied by Ladykat, Angelique Brando (Marlon Brando's daughter), Leyla and Tatiana, two beautiful Russians, and took a shuttle to the Majestic pontoon. **Guillermo del Toro** welcomed us and showed us around his private party. Since then, we've always had a special relationship with the master of fantasy cinema, who has collected 4 Oscars.

Solene and I were at a party. After putting on her Ladykat mask, she came and sat down next to me. **Benicio del Toro** and Eva Herzigova joined us. We had thus moved the VIP area around us. Ben supported us during the filming of the Kat Ladies pilot, in 2017, with Maria Sanchez and international ladies.

When I met **Elton John** in Paris, he was wearing a fluorescent orange leather suit adapted to his grey metal convertible. He introduced me to his musicians and their families. When we met again in Cannes, during a Black Chopard party (all was black, even Marilyn Monroe dress), he said to me: *Your name is too complicated. AZ it's easy.* Since then, I have been AZ for the American public and it's easier. It's a wonderful gift from such a great star. From Cannes to Saint Tropez, we have collected memories. Mainly, I am very lucky to have attended his show during a Chopard dinner. A piano, a microphone and Elton John's voice. Sublime!

Opposite page: photo shooting with the swedish top model **Victoria Silvstedt** at the Eden Roc Palace. A smily picture shot by Nicolas Moutte.

It was the handsome Bernard Giraudeau who made me enter my first party, in 1985. It was an evening organized by Première magazine where I was welcomed by **Frederic Mitterrand**. He is the nephew of François Mitterrand, who was President of France from 1981 to 1995.

We met several times. When I shot his picture posing with Ladykat, in 2006, we have no idea that it will be published in Les Inrocks magazine when he was appointed Minister of Culture, in 2009.

After I participed to a shooting with the great Helmut Newton, we went with all the team to a TV show with Frederic Mitterand and Arielle Dombasle as presenters. It was an astounding party with Coccinelle, one of the first trans women in the public eye

In 2011, Anne & Alain asked him to officially organize the first venue at Cannes of Joseph Jackson, the father of the King of Pop. He refused, telling us: That man was too mean to his son. Today, our books about the Cannes Film Festival often appear side by side.

Anne Gomis poses with **Chris Tucker**, the American actor of *Rush Hour*, who came to support the OFF de Cannes partners Tiffany McCall for some prestigious fashion catwalks in Carlton lounge. Like many American actors, he's very cool and played the game of joining all the models dressed in red on stage, himself wearing a red jacket.

I had read **Marilyn Manson's** biography a few months before I met the famous death metal singer. Knowing his sense of provocation, I gently teased him:

- Hey Brian, (his real name is Brian Warner), you wear a lens and I have two. We were in the Carlton celebrity bar. He then asked me if I wanted to see his wife's breasts. We joke at length, and I find myself with the VIP bracelet allowing me to attend the Dita von Teese Show in a glass of champagne. The short video posted on Myspace will exceed 100,000 views and bring visibility to our activities.

After her show, we have a drink with the beautiful Dita, and I discover a shy young woman who doesn't know where to put her purse. A delicious and very well-mannered woman.

This encounter with the Antichrist Superstar will allow me to rub shoulders with the Jackson family. Indeed, joking with this brilliant, intelligent man with a great sense of humor would earn me notoriety and respect from the Carlton's security service and the manager of the Celebrity Bar. So it was that, a few years later, in 2010, when we were looking for an exceptional venue to organize the OFF de Cannes ceremony, the establishment made available to us, free of charge, the Petit Bar du Carlton, for two hours. That's how we were approached by the Jackson Family Foundation.

Meeting **La Toya Jackson** is first and foremost surprising, as it's like seeing a female Michael Jackson in a blond wig. During her visit to Villa Oxygene, she agreed to cast her hands before slipping in among the guests. The eldest in her family, she is a singer, actress and a strong personality with a strong character who posed in Playboy magazine in March 1989. With Amir Bayyan, she co-wrote the famous song Reggae Night, which was given to Jimmy Cliff for release in 1983 and many songs with her brothers. In 1991, she publishes the autobiography "Jackson Story" (original title: La Toya: Growing Up in the Jackson Family).

Following Alain's meetings with Simon Sahouri, President of the Jackson Family Foundation, and Marco Derhi, President of Clean and film producer, in May 2010, and their meeting in Marseille a few weeks later, Alain Zirah and Anne Gomis are very proud to have been asked by the Jackson Family Foundation, and then mandated by Joseph Walter Jackson, patriarch of the first musical family, to organize the first visit of the Jackson family to Cannes. The father of the King of Pop, who died tragically on June 25, 2009 at the age of 50, was welcomed to Villa Oxygene by Richard Nilsson. He came with Dieter Wiesner, Michael and Janet Jackson's manager, as well as Simon Sahouri and Marco Derhy. Joseph Jackson explained to Alain: "my son was the greatest American dancer. There was Fred Astaire, Gene Kelly and Michael Jackson!"

According to Anne Gomis' perseverance, we had been commissioned in 2011 by **Joseph Walter Jackson**, patriarch of the first musical family. This gave us credibility to contact the most famous French TV presenter as Michel Drucker (France 2), Michel Denisot (Canal+) and various personalities and medias for his first visit to Cannes. About thirty of us could participate in his private conference to announce the launch of the first Michael Jackson Museum in Gary, Indiana, and the construction of a Happy Land park in Ho Chi Minh city, in Vietnam. The budget was 2 billion dollars. Michael Jackson and the Jackson Five were considered by their father as dancers. "I was strict with them as your French director of the Opera de Paris, that's all!" Alain and Anne met him several times and learned from him a lot about rigor and perseverance. Always seek to be the best. "The father of the King of Pop remembered us things about segregation in the sixties. You had to be strict to be recognize and to work with the best in each part of the musical industry!" And all his children are at the top level of the industry.

WIKIPÉDIA
L'encyclopédie libre

Following the OFF DE CANNES July 14, 2021 Garden Party held at the Palais Clément Massier, the team is delighted to discover its presentation on Wikipedia in early 2022. This recognition is a token of the seriousness and perseverance of an organization that has been working for over 15 years to help artists, particularly young artists, produce their projects.

The OFF de Cannes awards "the talents of tomorrow" through an international competition. The event takes place every year in Cannes (Alpes-Maritimes, Provence-Alpes-Côte d'Azur, France) on the same dates as the Cannes Film Festival (second half of May). The 9,000 artists discovered since 2005 are helped to move from the local to the international level. Their work is showcased during the eleven days of the Cannes Festival. The talents showcased have no connection with the official Cannes Festival selection because they are too avant-garde or don't fit into the categories in the running.

The main events take place in prestigious venues: Hôtel Majestic Barrière and Hôtel Carltons on the Croisette promenade in Cannes, Palais Clément Massier in Golfe-Juan: fashion shows, artists' exhibitions, literary salons, writers' signings, artistic meetings, musical showcases, short-film screenings.

Les OFF de Cannes was founded in May 2005 by Alain Zirah, a multi-faceted artist (photographer, writer, director, hypnotic painter). He was joined in 2011 by Anne Gomis, director and artist agent. Since its inception, the OFF de Cannes has benefited from the support of celebrities such as director Emir Kusturica, double Palme d'Or winner and patron in 2007, director Jan Kounen and the Partouche group in 2008, writer Paulo Coelho in 2009, Paul-Loup Sulitzer in 2019 and the Jackson Family, represented by Joseph Walter Jackson, in 2011... The sponsors of the 2021 edition are Eliot Cohen, founder of Red Bus Recording Studios4 in London, and TV host Danièle Gilbert.

The OFF de Cannes festival are broadcast in many countries, including the UK, the Netherlands, Brazil, India, Bangladesh, the USA, the Philippines, Congo and Iran.

Courtesy of Wikipedia

Preity Uupala (Miss India), Olympia Gellini (Family Film Awards), Alain Zirah, Steven Nia (Avenger: Endgame), Anne Gomis in Carlton Bar of the Celebrities. (In Interview above)

Organisation

The OFF de Cannes producers are Alain Zirah and Anne Gomis.

Alain Zirah, a multi-faceted artist, was the recipient of a 2015 Who's Who Wordwide Award in the United States. He has also received several awards for his works, including the 2016 Art Freedom Prize, for his novel Blood on Red Carpet awarded in Paris, and the Prix des Femmes de Lithe Litho awarded at Le Castellet in the Var in 2019. His film credits include the 2013 film *Forbidden Visions* with Afida Turner and the *Kat Ladies* series episodes.
In 2020, he won two awards at the WOW Awards in London, including Best Artist 2020. The Prix Lithe Litho 2022 was awarded to him for his body of literary work by the team at the medieval village of Le Castellet. In 2023, he received the Superstar Awards for Best NFT from the Superstar Art Foundation (Dallas, USA) for his digital works.

Anne Gomis joined the organization in 2011 as co-producer and manager. In the music field, she helped the Marseilles most famous rap group IAM obtain its label and open for Madonna in 1990 at Bercy. Organizing multi-ethnic musical evenings in Marseille with her mother Helene Gomis, she set up the Miss Black and Miss Night contests. She co-wrote and co-directed the screenplay for the feature film *Forbidden Visions* in 2013. She joined the OFF de Cannes in 2011, then became co-producer of the Family Films Awards for Dr. Olympia A. Gellini with Alain Zirah, in 2016. Both become members of the World Film Institute (Beverly Hills) in 2021.

> The team with Eliot Cohen (Red Bus Studios) and Angelique Brando in Majestic.

Fox'eye
crédit photo

Scope and influence of OFF de Cannes

Since 2005, OFF de Cannes has been helping artists, facilitating their meetings with professionals to whom they present their projects. After being selected during the Grand Concours International du Web and showcased at a ceremony in Cannes, OFF de Cannes accompanies them through to completion of their projects.

The OFF de Cannes brings international visibility to these artists and thus responds to the slogan "We don't make events, we write legends".

The Great International Web Contest

This competition, founded by Anne Gomis, complements the OFF de Cannes festival to select the best and most avant-garde artists in each artistic discipline: Cinema (directors/actors), Music, Dance, Writing, Fashion (stylists, models, photographers), Visual Arts (photography, painting, sculpture).

The jury is made up of professionals, including Max Howard (producer of *The Lion King*), Alain Reeves (composer), Jay Shindell (SFX supervisor for Steven Spielberg) and Steven Nia (SFX for *Avengers Endgame*). A committee pre-selects three artists per category, also considering the number of "likes" from Internet users. The shortlisted artists will then be presented to the jury for final selection. The jury for the 2021 ceremony was made up of three presidents: Bruno Chatelin, co-founder of Filmfestivals and Owner consultant of the Major Buzz Factory communications agency, Olympia A. Gellini, founder of the World Film Institute and Richard Guedj, actor and director of actors on the 17 years French series *Plus belle la vie*.

WHAT MOVES YOU, MAKES YOU*

Spike Lee et son stylo Meisterstück.
Incite à la réflexion depuis 1986.

Very famous French writer and business man, **Paul-Loup Sulitzer** was the youngest French CEO at 21. His books in a new literary genre: the «financial western». are bestsellers as Money, Cash, Fortune, and the Green King. They have been translated into over 40 languages and sold more than 40 million copies. He was the 2019 OFF de Cannes patron with his partner Supriya Ansuya Devi Rathoar. Anne Gomis saved his life in Monaco after he had a heart attack during the Monaco Formula 1 Grand Prix.

OFF DE CANNES 2018 - 2020

ARTISTS & ECOLOGY

Originally, since 2011, Alain Zirah and Anne Gomis used to come every year to the Cannes International Film Festival, where the organize the Great International Web Contest to discover new talents.

On Friday 2018 May 11 and Sunday May 13, the tea-room called *Autour D'un Livre*, at rue Bivouac Napoléon near the Palais du Festival, invited writers who published books about Cannes festival. The former president of the Cannes Film Festival, now retired, Gilles Jacob tells 40 years in his Cannes Festival Lovers' Dictionary, and Alain Zirah recounts anecdotes in his book Cannes Festival Backstage. After the autograph signing and presentation by Anne Gomis, a cross-interview organized by the two producers allows Gilles Jacob to answer Alain Zirah's questions to journalist Patrice Caillet for the Radio du cinema in Cannes.

radioducinema.com

They are very close to ecology since their childhood. Anne as African princess worked several years to bring renewable energies to the population in her villages. Alain made his first movie at 14 when he was in high school. After meetings with professionals an engineer, they begin to talk of these essential subjects to show Cannes festival is not a superficial place.

The idea was to put the spotlight on singers and musicians, writers, stylists and models, and painters to give strong messages about ecology, the fight against global warming and the proliferation of plastic in developing countries.

OFF DE CANNES 2018

The shortlisted artists of the 2018 Great International Web Contest meet in the champagne bar Le BIVOUAC. The assembled media discover the eclectic artists highlighted by this new edition. Fabio Rubio, Le Mans; Melvin Burrus, screenwriter from Tokyo; Sentya Routouang Miss Canada, Sophie Levine, model from London; Anne Gomis; Anne Laure assistant to Anne Gomis, Olympia Gellini from the Family Awards, Beverly Hills, USA; Alain Zirah; Prisca Fagnoni, stylist; Enoka Fonseca, Stylist from Sri Lanka, Riina Seize, model, Devy Man, director and sound designer, Paris; Candice Maury, model from Geneva, Switzerland; Michel Anthony, sculptor, the actress of Halidi M'Sa, dancers Karen Agopian Andre Lenzi, Lame d'Orient.

MISS FILM FESTIVAL INTERNATIONAL

GSF AWARDS/OFF DE CANNES GALA DINNER

On Saturday May 19, many guests gathered in the Grand Salon of the Intercontinental Carlton Cannes for the GSF /Off De Cannes/ Miss Film Festival International gala dinner. Many of the media were present to watch the prestigious fashion shows in the luxurious gilded setting of the Croisette's most sought-after palace. Accompanied by Carolien ter Linden (Pasarella Moda) and stylist Prisca Fanogny, Alain and Anne announced the winners.

The winners of the 2018 Great International OFF de Cannes Web Contest are:

Category Films:
"OFF de Cannes Grand Prize for films 2018" to **Naïs Graziani** for her beautiful touching short film *La Nuit*.
Halidi M'Sa is particularly fond of his short film with Anysia Lou, *Seule/Alone*.
The OFF de Cannes' jury for the 2018 ceremony awarded the " International Grand Prize of documentary" to **Germaine McCormack-Kos** for her report on cancer *Walk on the Wide Side*.

THE 2018 WINNERS GREAT INTERNATIONAL OFF CANNES FESTIVAL'S CONTEST

Cannes festival ex-president Gilles Jacob and Alain Zirah, writers were selected in dedication for their books about Cannes festival then in a crossed interview for Cannes TV and radio.
Alain Zirah & Anne Gomis with the artists in Carlton palace.

The winners of the 2018 edition of Great International Contest for OFF Cannes festival were receivein in a vin & champagne bar *Le Bivouac* on la Croisette before the *Intercontinental Carlton* ballroom for GSF/OFF Cannes Festival Gala.

THE WINNERS OF THE GREAT INTERNATIONAL WEB CONTEST AT CARLTON'S GSF GALA 2018

Category Music:

OFF de Cannes Grand Prize of Music 2018 to the lyrical singer **Vanina Aronica** for her breathtaking performance of the *Adagio*.

We fell in love with the Swedish DJ **Tim Bergling aka AVICII** who died suddenly at the age of 28 and award him the OFF de Cannes' coup de coeur.

Category Dance:

"Off de Cannes 2018 Grand Prize of Dance" to the duo **Lame d'Orient** by André Lenzi and Karen Agopian for the originality of their shows with belly dance and martial arts.

Category Fashion:

"The 2018 OFF de Cannes Fashion Grand Prize" is awarded to the fashion designer **Enoka Fonseka** for the glamour of her creations, with which she climbed nine steps on the Cannes red carpet, this year.

The Model of the Year "OFF de Cannes Grand Prize 2018" is awarded to **Sentya Routouang**, who was already awarded the title of Miss Style Canada 2018 this year.

A special OFF de Cannes "Coup de coeur" 2018 for the Make Up Artist **Dain Yoon** about "*My Modern Met*" and her astounding way of disappearing into her own landscape.

Category Plastic Arts:

The 2018 OFF de Cannes International Grand Prize of Fine Arts is awarded to **Jasmina Susak**, a fantastic graphic designer, for her masterful lesson in drawing Wonder Woman and our favorite characters.

The 2018 OFF de Cannes "Coup de cœur" is awarded to **Bianca de Lestrange,** a fashionista graphic designer and storyboarder.

Bloggers Category:

Hugo Mayer receives the 2018 OFF de Cannes International Grand Prize for his "*Blogreporter*" work during 10 years as a blogger and for his new and famous *Cannes Blog*.

Alain Zirah, Anne Gomis and **Olympia A. Gellini**, official OFF de Cannes festival partners and producers, also announced in Radisson Blu Rooftop...
the winners of the 22nd FAMILY FILM AWARDS:
Best actor: Johnny Depp for Pirate of the Caribbean.
Best Actress: Gal Gadot for Wonder Woman.
Best film: Wonder Woman by Patty Jenkins.

The OFF de Cannes crew with the First Lady of France, **Carla Bruni-Sarkozy** at Majestic before the opening of the event. (Sophie Levine, André Lenzi, Prisca Fagnony, Angelica Rutigliano, Sentya Routouang, Anne Gomis, Carla Bruni-Sarkozy, Alain Zirah)

OFF DE CANNES 2019

AMBITIOUS PROJECTS

The year 2019 also made a retrospective of the various OFF de Cannes festival editions, and the announcement of a major event for the 15th anniversary, in May 2020. The aim is to introduce the OFF de Cannes on mainstream national channels, to make a lasting impression and build audience loyalty this year and years to come.

After national partnerships with Annecy OFF (Annecy) and Art Freedom (Paris), new partnerships since 2016 give the Great International Web Contest a new international scope, notably with Tiffany Red Carpet (New York), Bakana Events (Paris), Family Film Awards (Los Angeles) and Global Short Film Awards (New York).

Other partnerships will further consolidate its reputation. Numerous meetings are planned in Marseille, Annecy and Paris, as well as in New York and Los Angeles, to advance various current projects. Several articles have been published in the media on the Carribean Indies, notably by our partner PEOPLE Alizés Mag. So, the series might be shoot in Guadeloupe, Saint Bart and Saint Martin. Alain went in Saint Barth and Saint Martin, in 2016, for scouting.

The OFF de Cannes Festival are talented discoverers who are at the forefront of the Cannes Film Festival and are preparing the films that will be in the spotlight tomorrow. The famous writer and businessman Paul-Loup Sulitzer takes the head of the events as OFF de Cannes festival's godfather. Alain Zirah, founder of the OFF de Cannes festival and Anne Gomis, are organizing the "Great International Web Contest" with a jury of professionals chaired by the President Dr. Olympia A. Gellini, founder of the World Film Institute and Family Films Awards, composed of Steven Nia, chairman of Wardour studios (Avengers - Endgame), Aleah Leigh (Integrity Magazine), Eric Ferrer (concert pianist), Raghunath Manet, Judi Beecher (Armaguedon), the Ambassador "Bijou" and the famous Tony Stark.

After the announcement of the winners of the 2019 edition at the MAGNIFICENT evening on May 17 organized by Lady Dragon Productions in a luxurious villa on the heights of Cannes, the jury members accompanied by their guests Movin' Melvin Brown, Melvin Burrus and the Franco-Canadian producer Michel Zgarka (Hitlab) introduced the winners. The ceremony in Carlton was filmed by the video journalist Wanda Nicot (WNBG Magazine by Wanda) as well as Frantz for Maxflava and many other media.

THE 2019 WEB CONTEST AT CARLTON

May 23, the winners of the 2019 Great International Web Contest are:

Category Fashion: The 2019 OFF de Cannes International Fashion Grand Prize was awarded to **Serine Kurt** Fashion designer for the quality, originality and glamour of her creations and wedding dresses. She came with models wearing her creations for a catwalk.

Bloggers Category: The OFF de la Special Grand Prize 2019 for Blog was awarded to the sublime **Candice Maury** for her spicy Lips blog. She demonstrated her pimp up to dress women's legs.

Category Plastic Arts: The Grand Prize for Photography was awarded to **Fox Eye**, the photographer of the stars, for the quality of her artistic photos but also for her endearing personality, her big heart and her availability.

The 2019 OFF de Cannes International Grand Prize for fine arts was awarded to **Steven Neill**, for the quality of his portraits of stars, Indians but also portraits of women in the face of sensuality.

Category Literature: The 2019 OFF de Cannes Grand Prize for Literature was awarded to **François Darietto** for his first novel ReZo, which was presented by his wife.

The 2019 OFF de Cannes Grand Prize for Poetry was awarded to **Marly Ramos** (Salvador) for the sound of her writing in Portuguese.

Category Music: Two 2019 OFF de Cannes Grand Prize for music were awarded to **D-Lisha** for the originality of her voice and the quality of her video clip and to **Marina Delmonde** for the accuracy of her performances.
Lola, represented by her agent Danny Combaret, is the 2019 Music Favourite.

The 2019 Cannes Off International Film Grand Prize was awarded to **Alexandre Laugier** for his film "Amour-eux". This will certainly help him to produce and realize his new science fiction project.

Black Music

KOPZO
FAVELA
CERVEJA
DRAGON LADY PRODUCTIONS
MAGNIFICENT
RAINDANCE FILM FESTIVAL
SHAKING THE TREE

THE FAVORITES OFF 2019

Sensitive to the creativity of the many artists, the jury members awarded several Coup de Coeur Awards to talents shortlisted by the OFF de Cannes.

Pascal Lastrajoli was awarded the OFF de Cannes Coup de cœur 2019 for film. He explained on social networks how the OFF de Cannes Grand Prix 2018 enabled him to shoot a short film with Olivier Marchal and another one with David Halliday, the son of the famous French star Johnny Halliday.

Fashion designer **Prisca Fanogny** had already made a name for herself the previous year with shows and creations worn during the Cannes festival and receives the 2019 Coup de Cœur for Fashion.

The OFF de Cannes Coup de Coeur 2019 for Visual Arts was awarded to multidisciplinary artist **Valéria Douchky,** who like to paint, write with talent, but also showcase her pictorial works in original videos.

The Coup de Coeur 2019 for Music is awarded to little **Lola,** represented by her agent Danny Combaret.

Finally, **Marie Blanche Cordou** is the OFF de Cannes Coup de cœur for Books 2019 for the quality of her writing and her latest novel, as well as her dedication to organizing literary salons, festivals and meetings.

Many of the Carlton's guests, producers, actors, actresses and models join the team and the jury members in the International Carlton lounge for the inevitable selfies and group photos that are such trademarks, year after year, of the Cannes Film Festival.

In front of the cameras, Alain Zirah paid a moving posthumous tribute to the multi-talented director and artist **Philippe Carrese** who left too early, at the age of 63, a few days before the festival. Philippe had distinguished himself as a writer of «polar aioli» and a film director who had won several awards. It also pays tribute to Prodream writer and producer **Serge Uzan**. Ambassador Jessica also paid tribute to the American actor **Clement von Frankenstein** who died the day before the Cannes Film Festival at the age of 74. Three friends who will remain in the memories of the Cannes Film Festival.

Jean-Pierre Guillemou, Philippe Carrese, Jacques Brachet, Jean Maltese, Serge Uzan Patrick Lachaud, Clement von Frankenstein

After his showcase, on demand from Paul Loup Sulitzer, the camer singer **Prince Kestamg** received the Honor Awards for the originality of his happy song. Many Carlton guests, producers, actors, actresses and models come to join the team of the Cannes Film Festival to make the essential selfies. The Grand Prix was awarded at the Royal Covent of Saint Maximin, on June 21.

Some publications from RED CARPET MAGAZINE #38 Chicago)

20/20 CULTURE

WRAP

VARIETY

THE Hollywood REPORTER

es Market 2019

INTERNATIONAL FILM MARKET

FESTIVAL DE CANNES
12-23 mai 2020

C'est pas parce qu'on est confinés

qu'on doit devenir des cons finis !

Alas the year 2020 had been shocked by the covid pandemic. The world had stopped, and everything was cancelled. The lockdown during 51 days from March 15th changed all mindset. Alain Zirah & Anne Gomis decided to shoot some shows for YouTube. It was called 20/20 CULTURE. They made 3 shows. Cannes Festival was totally cancelled. So, for the episode #4 the decided to play a show called "Cannes festival happens in Marseilles". It was a time of transformation when everyone had to learn how to adapt and change his mindset.

Then, the team decided to rent a cool office in Blackfeeling radio, a station in the city of Marseilles where they organized some WebTV shows with international partners and some musical showcases.

Bl@ckfeeling Radio
le meilleur de la Black Music
sur jim...eeling.com

Bl@ckfeeling Radio
le meilleur de la Black Music
...blackfeeling...m

2020 OFF DE CANNES

The projects for 2020 OFF de Cannes would have been quite important. They need someone to represent the team all over the world and during the 2020 Cannes festival, in May, to honor the winners of the Great International Web Contest. The flashes were supposed to crackle during the 15th OFF de Cannes anniversary... But everything was cancelled and close.

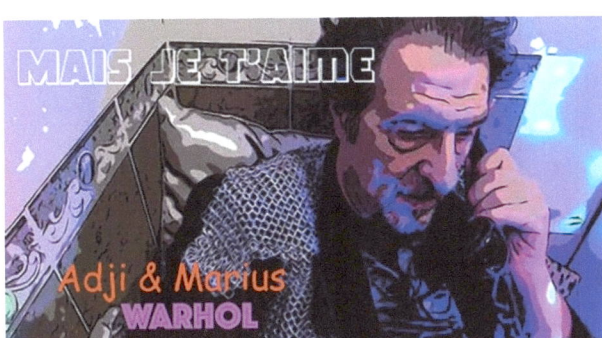

The team had been proud to annonce that the new OFF de Cannes ambassadress was a pure Iranian diamond living in Netherland, inside Europa. The beautiful **Sara Hassany** aka Sara Star won two crowns in South Africa as Mrs Netherland International 2018 and Top Model Europa 2018 & 2019. Then Best Model of Europe in Spain in 2019. But the lights of Cannes festival stayed off. Everything had been cancelled.

I share my time between cinema, music, fashion, fine arts and books.

1. What do you do for a living?

I'm an artist who decided, in 2005, to open my mind to visionary perspectives. I founded OFF Cannes Festival and discover avant-gardist new talents in cinema, music, blog, fashion and fine arts. With these I produce and direct films, fantasy fictions, and publish books. My 6th one will be publish next month with the title *Forbidden to Men/Interdit aux Hommes*. I'm a winning artist living in France (receiver of 2015 Who's who Worldwide UNESCO Award" and 2016 Prix Art Freedom for my book *Blood on the Red Carpet/ Du Sang sur le Tapis Rouge*. I also get a Price in 2013 for my 30 years of photography exhibitions. Actually, I'm working on digital series called *Kat Ladies*, about the Girl Power and just came back from Cannes where Anne Gomis and I announced the winners of our Great International Contest on the Web for 2018 OFF Cannes Festival in Intercontinental Carlton.

photo Franz Fox Kennedy

MISS FILM FESTIVAL INTERNATIONAL

Photo Ko Kok

2. How would you describe what you do?

I share my time between several projects but all the things go together. Sometimes I feel like a conductor of a Philharmonic and sometimes I'm just an orchestra man. In fact I have good visions of stories and just choose which medium suits to express the best feelings. Is it writing a story or drawing, painting, shooting photography or fight searching funds to make a film. There are not separate arts. But in France, the people expect you stay into a unique box. If you write stories, you might only be a writer. And the difficulties are production but also distribution. If you are not someone' son, you can't get millions of fans. It's the reason why I created OFF Cannes Festival to assemble multidisciplinary artists because we all work on different projects and develop a spatial vision of each ones. We must dream with open eyes to make them come true. And working in these different fields makes me feel more complete as an artist. A complete artist.

3. What does your work entail?

My work entails to practice every day, writing, shooting photos or editing films. And to keep humility. To have a magical crazy life I don't sleep so much. Life changes these last years with smartphones and social networks. We have several jobs a day and night. Writing mails, the morning, cruising to the meetings, the afternoon, editing photos before sending them to the virtual/ real friends the evening and writing books the night. But there are no rules. Working on International project is a wonderful opportunity to discover people from new countries and different cultures.

photo Christian Pinson

4. What's a typical work week like?

I can't really say that I have a typical work week. I had in the past and am very happy to wake up each morning without any idea of what my week will look like. My week depends on my assignments (film shooting, photo shoots, writing books or promotion with dedicates, painting or organizing the next event in beautiful places. I try to be at the right place, in the right time with the right people. My magical life allowed me to take the most beautiful women in my arms, with champagne, in prestigious place with good music. Thanks God, life is good.

5. How did you get started?

I started writing some short stories and drawing comics before studying in Fine Arts school in Marseille where I was born. I choose to have an atypical formation and worked in a real estate company. But I was also a photographer for IMAPRESS agency. It was cool to shoot beauties in studio and meet celebrities before to shoot them. The agency sales my photos in different countries. So, I was on stage with David Bowie and sell photos to Japan. He was my huge star and model. I was very impressed that stars as Beyonce, Devon Aoki or David Guetta use my photos for their Wikipedia. Then, after a life in Paris, I decided to develop my artistic fiber. I went in Cannes festival till 1983 and realized I met several multitalented artists that couldn't enter in the specific categories of the International Film festival. different categories. The Web changes everything.

So, in 2005, I founded OFF Cannes Festival in Majestic where we presented a young American director, Mark W. Gray. Six years later, he gets an award as best director at New York festival.

In 2011, with Anne Gomis, we organize the Great International Web Contest. At the same time, I began to publish my book about Cannes Festival Backstage/Dans les coulisses du Festival de Cannes which was republished in its 2017 edition. During 71st Cannes Festival, I had a dedicate with Gilles Jacob, the President of Cannes Festival for 40 years, and we had a crossed interview. Then we announced the names of our winners in Carlton.

We met the legend of Hollywood, Dr Olympia Antonio Gellini, in 2016, and we produced and hosted him in Carlton for the XXth Family Film Awards. This year, for the third time, we announced the XXIIth Family Film Awards in a luxury wine and champagne bar in front of le Palais du festival. So we announced the winners, Johnny Depp and Gal Gadot as best actor and actress, and Wonder Woman as the best film. So, our partner, founder of World Film Institute and Olympia Awards, proposed us to meet the winners in LA and to begin the French Family Film Awards, next year.

photos: Tristan Authoserre

I was awarded in 2013 for photography in Paris where I lived for ten years, then in 2015 for Who's Who worldwide for 10 years of my activity within OFF Cannes Festival and in 2016 for my book *Blood on the Red Carpet/ Du Sang sur le Tapis Rouge* whose story begins with a serial killer in Cannes. Then I received the Prize *Cap sur l'Europe* (2019), the Femmes diploma Lithé Litho 2019 for my book *Forbidden to Men* and an Awards for lifetime literary achievement by the medieval village of Le Castellet in December 2022. So, I am very honored and proud to be recognize for the quality of my books.

Now, Google is my best friend. When you googlise my name, you get the best presentation I ever dreamed.

6. What do you like about what you do?

I like the opportunity to discover the world of different artists, meeting musicians, writers and directors, to learn from them, to be amazed everytime about how life is rich and surprising. Be curious is a real professional enrichment.

You got an idea in your bed, you write a short story in sofa or in the kitchen. You choose the good people and shoot videos. Then, when you see your film in theater with beautiful actresses talking your words to men, you receive incredible emotions. Each moment is unique and you have to fix the time with cameras, words or drawing. We, as people, have a limited life but our creations are eternal.

There are only 24 hours in a day! For Steven Sp)ielberg or yourself, it's always 24 hours. So, I have to deal with my schedule to do all the things in time. It's hard to manage everything and I don't like to be an orchestra man.

In France, making film is very difficult if you're not somebody's son. There is a cultural French exception, but the public funds only go to the same circle of people without ambition to make French comedy only for French audience. It's very difficult for young artists to get a big audience or international audience, even with YouTube and the social networks. I always be very mystic and that feelings grow up with the years. Becoming older brings wisdom.

I would have like being as Puccini or Richard Wagner.

t's the reason why, today, I call all the artists, producers, distributors and TV broadcast to break the bad circle. Till 2005, I discovered many avant-gardist talents, and they don't get the good way to make their masterpiece. So, come with me, break the circle and express the best you can do. I break the circle when I created OFF Cannes Festival, a magic tool who permit to approach huge stars not as VIP but as artists 2018 and cast talents coming from different countries, with different colors and religions around next creations, original and unique. Actually, directors are similar as composer of classical music. If I lived two centuries before, I would have like being as Puccini or Richard Wagner.

I always put the women above men.

photo Michel Le Ho

9. What skills are needed to do this?

I love my job and love my life. I know how much I am lucky to do the job that I love. Do what you want, where you want, with the people you appreciate. It's fantastic. At the same time, all the artists wil tell you how much it's a hard work, because your brains are working H 24. To make your dreams come true, you need perseverance and patience. To convince people to follow you in crazy projects, you need to be charismatic but also megalomaniac.

10. What is most challenging about what you do?

As a film maker, it's very difficult to direct actors to become someone else and being themself at the same time. I like working and works as deep as possible to obtain the best images with the best emotions. Words are precious. It's a mystical way to use a sentence and the audience repeat it. Women are divine and give life while men fight with sports or wars. So, thinking of new ideas and fighting to bring a project until to its term, that is very challenging.

You must defend your ideas beaks and mails. And, of course, I learned to do not take account of the negative reviews. So many people are jealous or envious. You can't please everyone.

But, first essential thing, it's necessary to be passionate. Without passion, magical life is impossible. When you're an artist, your life is different. That's an artist's life.

In my films, I consider ideas, images, sounds and words are very important. And, of course, the story and the casting are essential. Meeting everyday new people, actresses and models –my digital series talk about the Girl Power and Black Power- is a fantastic motor for creativity. Women are my tools. In books, films, photography or paintings, I always put the women above men. I try to give the best of myself and to transmit the best ideas of humanity for the new generation.

11. What advice would you offer someone considering this career?

My dad gave me the only advise I could transmit. If you want success, you need working hard, two time more than others. Long time ago I met a man in Paris. He was a night watchman in a classy hotel. He explains me how years ago, in the 70's, he was a famous black singer as Tany Welck. He had a hit with Sexy Man. He teached me that I had to find my own sun. When you'll get your sun, keeps it in front of you and always walk in the direction of your own sun.

You must be authentic and tell the right words you kept inside your heart and soul. You can't effectively defend an idea to which you do not believe. That's what I learned very early. So, it's very rewarding to receive the applauses you deserve. I'm very happy when people tell me how much they were touched by the words in my books or films. I feel the messages and emotions and want to share with them. These are the most beautiful compliments and rewards an artist can get.

So, keep on being focused, work hard, study and every time you fall, learn a new way to raise again.
To create great things, don't wait but always do the best you can do. Sometimes it works, sometimes it doesn't. But as an artist, always keep your passion alive and growing day after day. Like a fire.

12. How much time off do you get?

We just came back from the Cannes Film Festival. It was deep and intense. With a sense of permanent euphoria. You meet lot of people. You are happy to see good friends from foreign countries, but you can't get a single minute of time off with them. You're like an animal in a hurricane. Everything goes too fast, for two weeks! You must make your elevator pitch in one minute before talking with other people. Your brain is every time in ebullition, and we conceive a lot of new projects a day. But I'm not sure I would appreciate been off more than a simple day without any creation. Even on the beach I write poetry or stories. That's how I wrote my books *God create Woman alike herself,* and the last one *Forbidden to Men.*

Alain Zirah by May-Panda (2017)

13. What else would you like people to know about your career?

Well, I have a life in real estate during 25 years with prestige luxury rental and promote 53 apartments building before to change everything in my life. And what's funny is that a lot of people can't imagine my past. Now, I hope to have the opportunity to shoot films in other languages in the future and in new countries (Egypt, India...)

Love is the Best Thing in the World

At school, my philosophy teacher, Ferdinand Lallemand, was an adventurer in its young life exploding deep water with Commandant Cousteau for searching vestiges of civilization of Atlantis. With him, I learned that you could change completely your life.

14. What is a common misconception people have about what you do?

Being an artist is being different. You see things the other people can't see, and you must understand other people who don't have such a chance. Some are jealous or criticized your job. But you must stay clean with serenity.

You communicate deeply about your naked soul because you give love around you and there's a special feeling inside you are shouting that you need love. All we need is love. The best thing in the world.

OFF DE CANNES 2008 / 2010
THE BEGINNING

How we created an event within the prestigious Cannes event

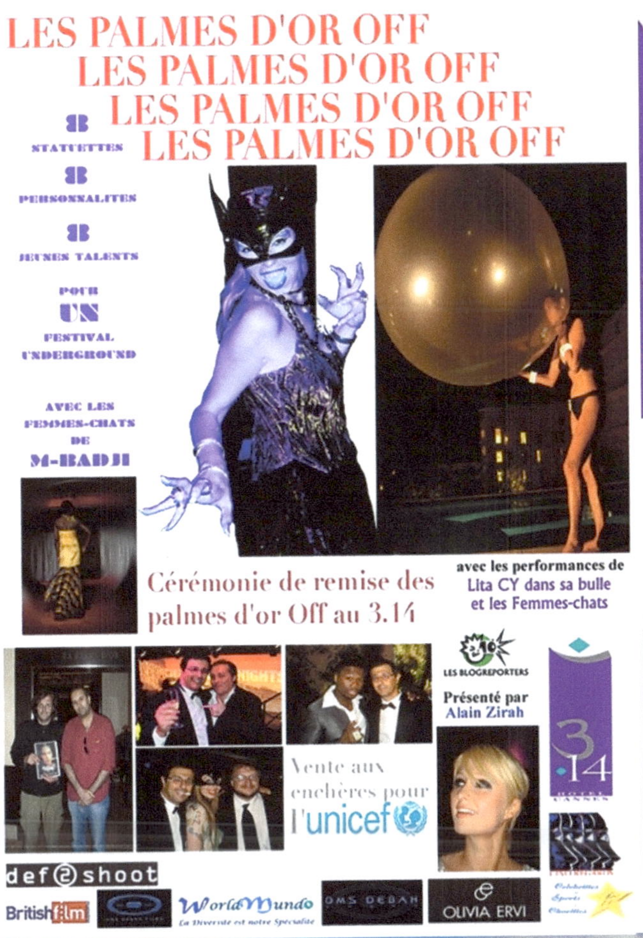

LES PALMES D'OR OFF
LES PALMES D'OR OFF
LES PALMES D'OR OFF
LES PALMES D'OR OFF
8 STATUETTES
8 PERSONNALITES
8 JEUNES TALENTS
POUR UN FESTIVAL UNDERGROUND
AVEC LES FEMMES-CHATS DE M-BADJI
Cérémonie de remise des palmes d'or Off au 3.14
avec les performances de Lita CY dans sa bulle et les Femmes-chats
LES BLOGREPORTERS
Présenté par Alain Zirah
Vente aux enchères pour l'unicef
def2shoot
BritishFilm
WorldMundo
La Diversité est notre Spécialité
OLIVIA ERVI

BritishFilm
OLIVIA ERVI
WorldMundo
& ALAIN ZIRAH Présentent les
OFF 2008
FESTIVAL UNDERGROUND
avec les Femmes-chats de Mathy Badji
Vip INVITATION
LES OFF DE CANNES 2008
Hotel 3.14 le 22 Mai @ 19h
3.14 HOTEL CANNES
unicef
LADY in the Renaissance Bubble
61e
E CANNES

CARLTON
INTER-CONTINENTAL

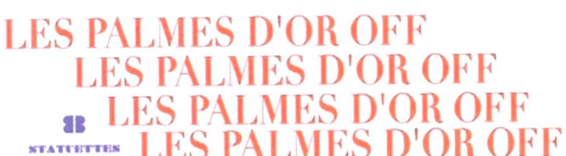

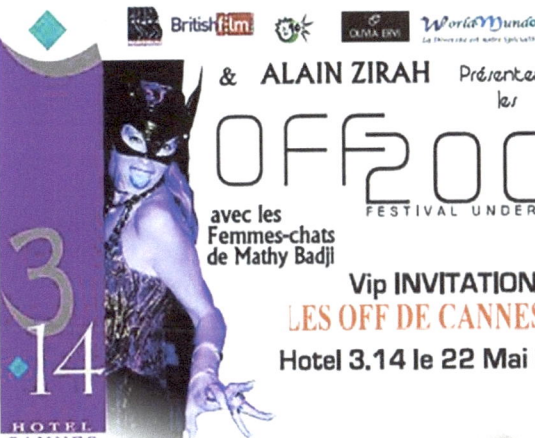

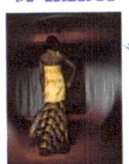

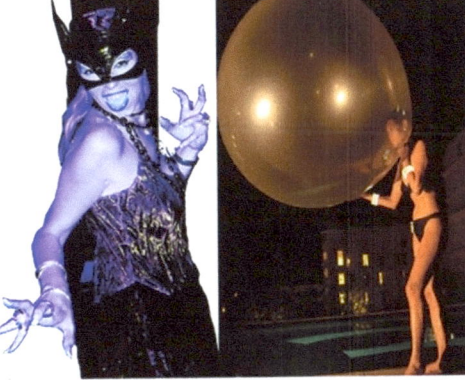

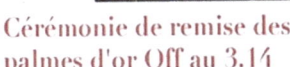

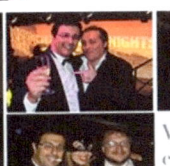

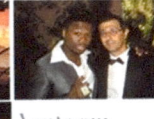

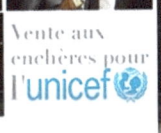

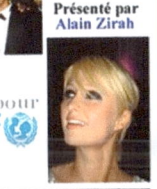

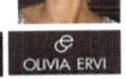

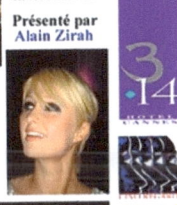

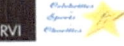

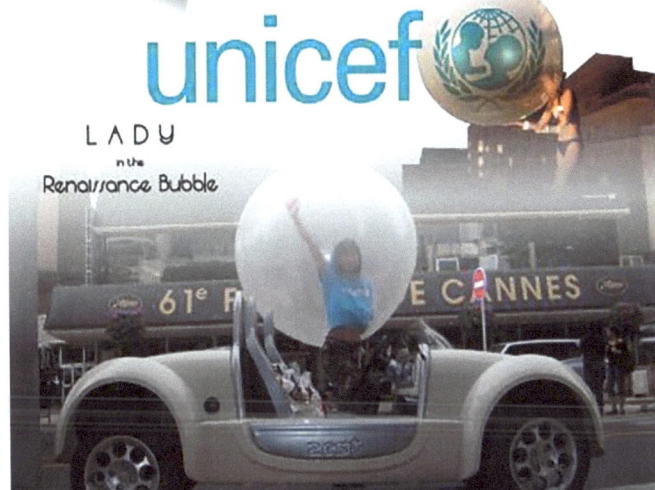

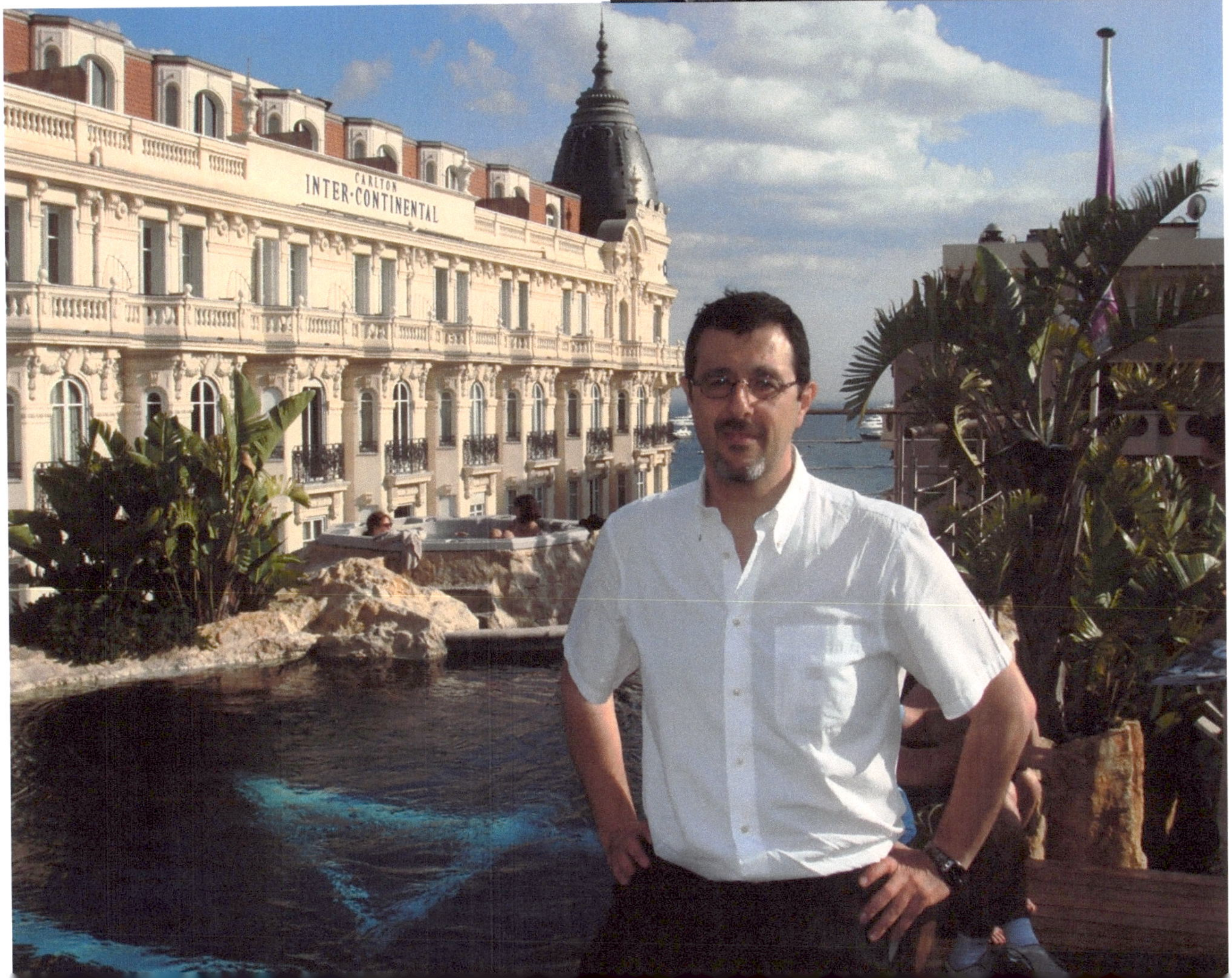

OFF DE CANNES 2008 / HOTEL 3.14

Photo : L. Racanelli

Photo : Mark-R

EVENT PRESENTATION

The purpose of the OFF de Cannes is to put into limelight young talents out of competition of the Cannes Festival. This event held during the Cannes Festival gives the opportunity to reward the participants of the most creative competition around the theme "Kat Ladies". Created by Alain Zirah in 2005, this ceremony celebrates its 4th birthday and is organized by the society named CINQ REGARDS. This event has already brought together many celebrities and enabled a substantial number of new talents to be discovered on the fringe of the world biggest cinema festival.

Further to this success, we renew this event in 2010. The competition will reward new talents creativity in various categories: cinema, photography, painting, blogs and fashion, every time with the "Kat Ladies" theme.

The OFF de Cannes Golden Kats are new statuettes created for the event by the Argentinean artist **Mark-R** and will be handed out by an international jury.

Set in the heart of Cannes, the «OFF de Cannes» Golden Kat Awards ceremony honors talent that is not in competition at the festival.

This unique event, created by Alain Zirah, is organized by French ONG CINQ REGARDS to spotlight a veritable breeding ground of new talent. Alain Zirah has been a regular at the Cannes Festival since May 1983 and, with his team, has been working on the OFF de Cannes event since 2005.

OFF DE CANNES 2008 / HOTEL 3.14

Above: Coach speech by Lydia Messeguer
Next page: With Marinella Cucciardi at the Intercontinental Carlton in Cannes.

2008, May 22nd

The OFF de Cannes team is invited to appear on Canal+'s Grand Journal. Michel Denisot, the boss of France's best-known TV show, really liked the concept created by Alain Zirah. He invited the team to appear on Grand Journal the following evening. An appointment was made. The next day, Alain Zirah and Mathy Badji headed to the Martinez, accompanied by Lydia Meseguer and Lita CY. Bad news: tonight, the set is occupied by Madonna, Sharon Stone, Jean-Claude Van Damme and Jane Birkin... The team doesn't give up and sends Lita to have the rag dolls signed by Madonna, Sharon Stone, Jean-Claude Van Damme and Jane Birkin... The personalized dolls will be auctioned off for UNICEF to benefit sick children during the evening ceremony, sponsored by Groupe Partouche.

This Thursday evening saw the 3rd edition of the Palmes d'Or des OFF de Cannes 2008 Awards ceremony, held in the sumptuous setting of the Hôtel 3.14 terrace. The aim of this event is to reward out-of-competition talent from the Cannes Film Festival. This celebration is the brainchild of Alain Zirah. Alain Zirah is a multi-faceted filmmaker and artist. He is also president of the Cinq Regards association, whose mission is to support and accompany film-related projects. Lydia Meseguer, branding coaching specialist and operation manager, was the mistress of ceremonies for the evening, accompanied by mentalist Raymi Phenix. Producers, directors, actors and artists of all kinds were on hand to witness this great evening. Numerous artists from the Croisette rounded out the entertainment with clowns and jugglers. Two Charlie Chaplin lookalikes were on hand to pay tribute to the 7th art.

The OFF de Cannes 2009 Golden Kats Awards ceremony will take place on Wednesday May 20, during a two-hour evening that will be shoot as TV show for web channels. For this 4th edition, 9 statuettes will be awarded by an international jury to reward the creativity of the young talents of 2009, highlighted in nine sections.

A new feature for 2009 will be a creativity contest, in which the winning directors will be able to edit their films live on iMacs provided by Apple. The OFF de Cannes 2009 trophies will be statuettes bearing the effigy of the Catwomen, created by Argentinian sculptor Mark-r. The ceremony will be followed by a fashion show led by the talented fashion designer Mathy Badji, who will present her latest creations on the cat-woman theme, as well as the young designers selected.

The OFF de Cannes Golden Kats Awards Ceremony is divided into four parts:
1/ Introductory speeches by members of the jury and the Kat Ladies, actresses playing for short film directed by Alain Zirah
2/ Fashion show organized and hosted by the talented young fashion designer Mathy Badji, winner of the OFF de Cannes 2008 Award.
3/ Jury awards the OFF de Cannes trophies to all the winners.
4/ Cocktails during which models, jury members and winners mingle with financiers, investors, producers, directors, actresses and actors.

Photos will be taken in front of the sponsor panel.

www.cinemaniac.fr

123

OFF DE CANNES EVENING PROGRAM

On Wednesday, 20TH of May, the fourth OFF de Cannes edition with the OFF de Cannes Party will start and take place on different TV channels live broadcast, on "ANBTV", "La Locale.TV" and "92TV".

The evening Kats d'Or Awards will take place in 4 parts:
Opening speech presenting members of the jury & the competition,

Prize giving "OFF de Cannes" by the members of the jury to all the winners.

Kat Ladies fashion show for the fashion winners, followed by the final Kat Ladies show by the young fashion creator **Mathy Badji,** followed by a musical showcase.

Cocktail during which models, members of the jury & winners mix up with finance people, investors, producers, actors & actresses.

The objective is to organize a top-quality event to be the reference.

Fashion designer Mathy Badji
Model Anastasia
Photo : Giancarlo

Fashion designer Mathy Badji
Model Simona Zampini
Photo : Salon des Miroirs – Paris

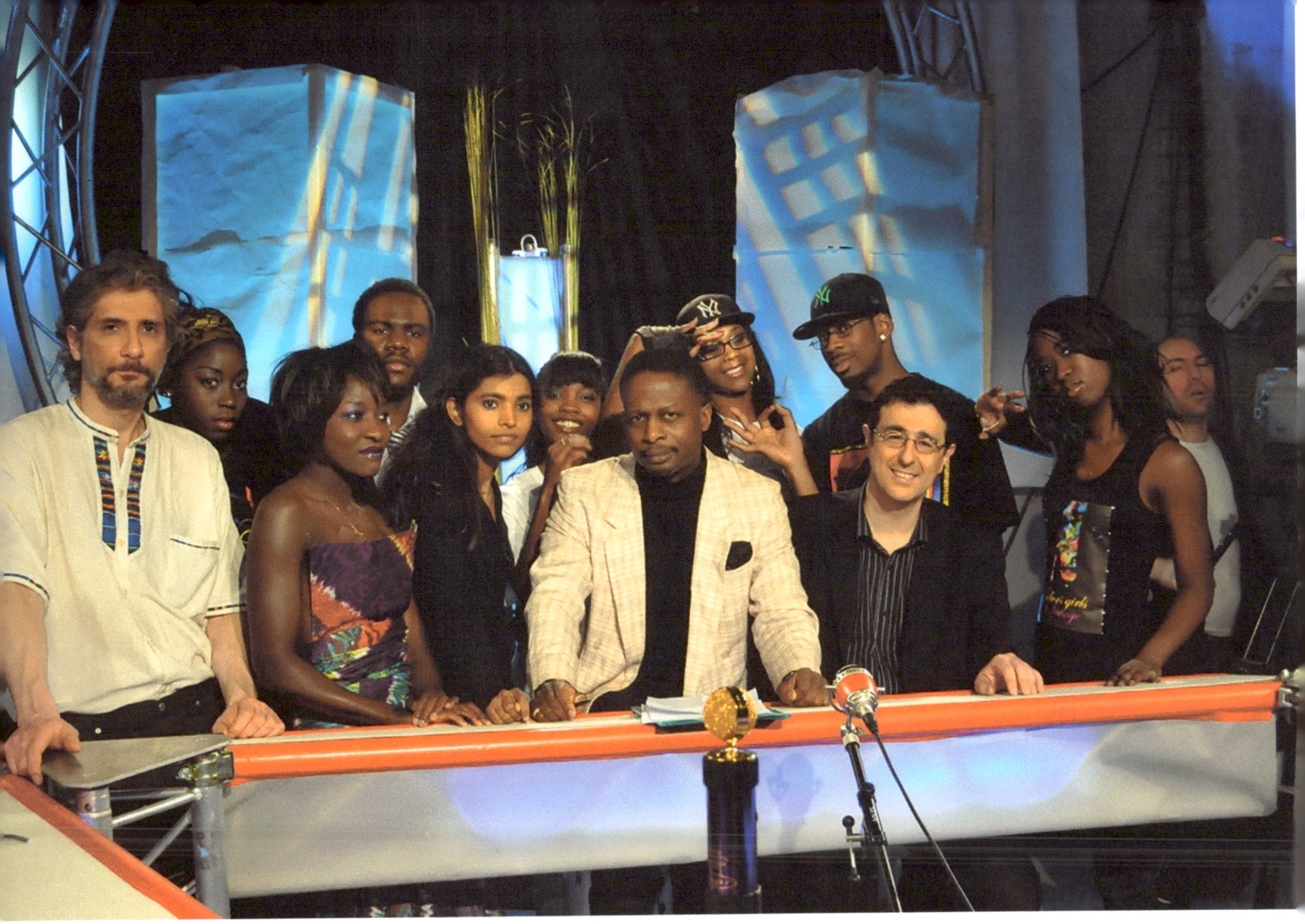

The famous french TV presenter Patrick Lachaud invited Alain Zirah, Mathy Badji and their team at La Locale TV to announce a special event in Ideal Hotel in Paris before the Cannes festival and the amazing Kat Ladies party.

Mode

Mathilde Badji

"Etre une femme, c'est une chance"

A 26 ans, Mathilde Badji est déjà une femme très décidée. Elle concrétise son rêve de petite fille, devenir styliste et créer des robes somptueuses, tout en gagnant sa vie comme vendeuse dans une boutique de vêtements, et en étant l'assistante d'autres couturiers. Un réalisme qui ne l'a pas empêchée de réaliser un premier défilé, à Issy-les-Moulineaux, très remarqué. Le journal Le Parisien lui a même consacré un article ! Née à Paris de parents sénégalais, Mathilde a gardé de ses origines un sens de la famille, une grande capacité à se faire des amis, ainsi qu'un goût certain pour le travail en indépendante...

Mathilde, quelle est votre formation?

J'ai un BEP-CAP, suivi d'un Bac Pro en VMA - Vêtements sur mesure et accessoires. Ensuite, je suis entrée à l'Ecole Formamod, pendant deux ans.

Vous avez choisi une voie risquée, la mode, où l'offre est déjà nombreuse...

Quand j'étais petite, je voulais être mécanicien, comme mon mon papa ! Mais quand j'ai grandi, j'ai changé d'avis : c'était trop salissant ! J'ai cherché une autre voie. Ma mère faisait de la couture en Afrique, un jour j'ai vu une photo d'elle, devant sa machine à coudre. J'ai eu envie de faire comme elle. Mes premiers modèles, c'étaient des robes que je cousais à la main, pour les barbies de ma petite sœur. J'avais 8 ans...

Avez-vous commencé à coudre ensuite des vêtements pour vous?

Non: je n'ai jamais osé coudre pour moi-même. Je cousais toujours pour les autres, et d'abord pour mes amies. Mon premier vêtement, c'était une robe pour la petite fille que ma maman gardait, Victoria, qui avait 5 ans : une petite robe en laine de tweed.

Qu'est-ce qui vous plait dans ce métier de créatrice de mode?

C'est de laisser son imagination voguer sans se mettre de barrières... Quand on crée, on est un peu dans une bulle, on a l'impression de rentrer dans une quatrième dimension! On a envie de le voir porté, on a la satisfaction de voir son œuvre terminée.

Comment vous vient l'inspiration?

Les idées sont partout! Au coin de la rue, quand je vais chercher la baguette le matin, quelque chose peut faire tilt ! Et les tissus africains m'inspirent beaucoup. J'aime beaucoup les betchos, les pagnes, les bimbims... Ce qui m'attire, ce sont les couleurs. J'aime beaucoup les couleurs, et les tissus africains sont très colorés.

Vous êtes née et vous vivez à Paris: quel contact avez-vous, ici, avec la mode africaine ?

C'est par nos mères d'abord, quand elles vont à des fêtes, à des mariages. Les femmes africaines, en France, essayent de garder les coutumes de là-bas. Quand on est invitée, il faut être la plus élégante possible, avoir un nouveau vêtement, une nouvelle coiffure... La femme africaine veut être très élégante, pour elle-même, et pour le regard des autres. Ma mère m'a appris à être correctement habillée. Même aujourd'hui, alors que j'ai 26 ans, elle me dit encore parfois : *"Pourquoi tu es habillée comme ci, ou comme ça?"*!

Allez-vous souvent en Afrique?

Je ne suis allée qu'une fois en Afrique : c'était en 1996, au Sénégal. Mais j'ai été très attirée par tout ce que j'ai vu là-bas. Je suis allée à Dakar, et en Casamance, dans le village natal de mes parents. C'était très beau, la campagne très verte, les maisons en terre cuite. J'avais l'impression de vivre un siècle en arrière! C'est assez bizarre, mais je suis plus attirée par les choses anciennes que modernes... Je suis tombée complètement amoureuse du Sénégal, et la seule chose qui me retient d'y retourner, ce sont les finances!

Voyez-vous une différence entre les femmes africaines et européennes pour leur rapport à la mode ?

On peut très bien allier la mode africaine avec la mode occidentale. Par exemple, décliner un tissu africain avec une coupe à l'occidentale. Ce mélange, ce melting-pot, est très courant. Sinon, la principale différence que je vois, c'est que les parisiens n'osent pas les couleurs. Ils ont des codes. Par exemple, en hiver, ils vont porter des couleurs sombres. Mais ça n'est pas une raison, parce que c'est l'hiver! Au contraire, je crois qu'une Européenne doit porter des couleurs. Ca égaye son visage, et l'autre qui est en face ! Moi, que ce soit l'été ou l'hiver, je porte toujours des couleurs!

Pourquoi selon vous est-ce important pour une femme d'être bien habillée?

Nous sommes des femmes. Nous avons le choix. Le code vestimentaire des hommes est très limité : ce sont des chemises et des pantalons. Nous, avec les courbes et les formes que nous avons, nous avons la possibilité d'une multitude de vêtements, par rapport aux hommes. Etre une femme, c'est une chance !

Portez-vous les tenues que vous créez?

Comme beaucoup de créateurs, je ne porte pas mes propres créations! Sauf pour des occasions. ■

Contact: mabadji@hotmail.com

Propos recueillis par Nadia Khouri-Dagher

N°449 AMINA 2007

18

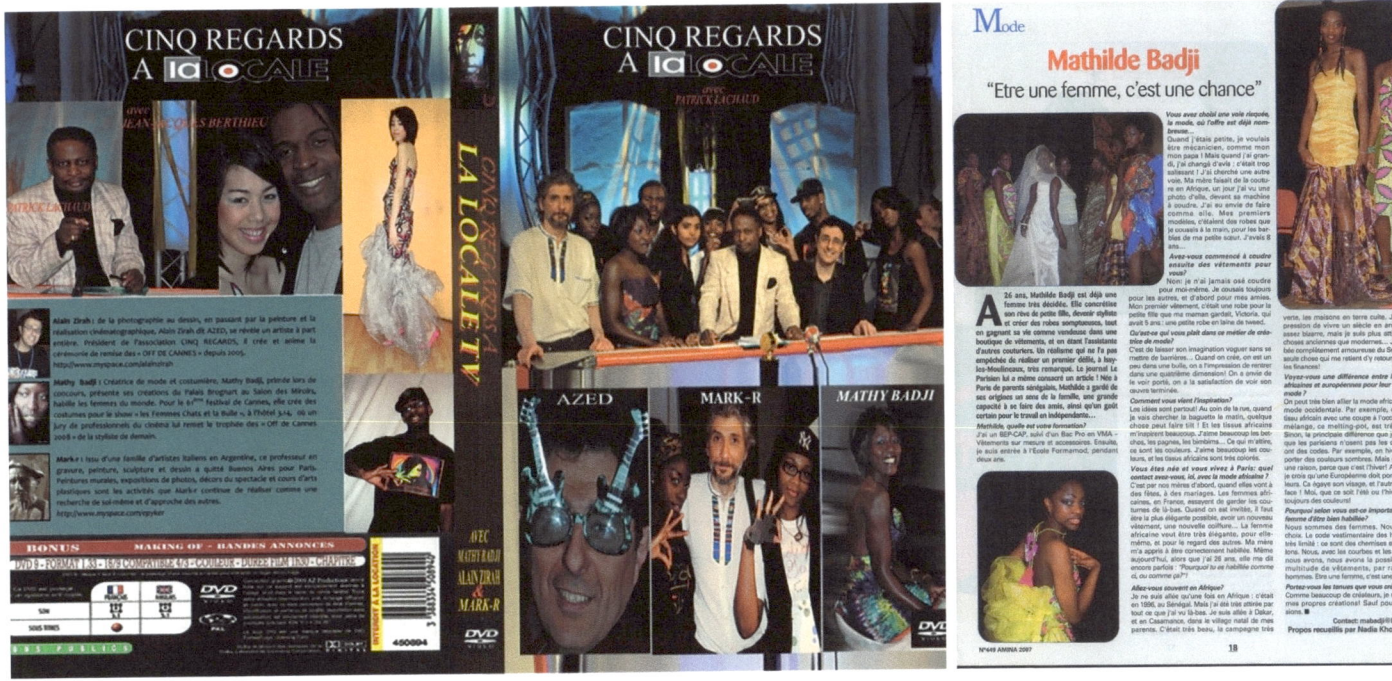

The Locale TV show, co-hosted by Patrick Lachaud and Mathy Badji, got Parisians talking about the dresses created by the talentuous designer.

The international jury composed of **Hugo Mayer**, actor and blogger, **Lydia Meseguer**, certified branding coach, **Solene Guionnet**, actress and painter, **Raymi Phenix**, mentalist, **Terence Doyle**, editor-in-chief of British Films Magazine, **Olivia Ervi**, designer in Cannes, **Mark W. Gray**, American director, and **Nida Wakim**, Lebanese director, presented the golden palms entitled OFF de Cannes 2008 to the young talents discovered during this festival.

Lady and the Renaissance Bubble has put on a show that will be remembered with Lita CY in her bubble surrounded by the five female cats dressed with crazy outfits by the designer Mathy Badji, assisted by Alexis Faure, and made up by Philippe Podevyne and Melanie Laurent. Devy Man made the poster and shot some images that will be set to music by Maurice Eliam. Everyone appreciates the video with a remarkable electro sound.

OFF DE CANNES 2008 / HOTEL 3.14

2008, May 22

The Cannes OFF team was invited to the *Grand Journal de Canal+*. Michel Denisot, the owner of the most famous French TV show, really liked the concept created by Alain Zirah. He suggested that the team spend the next evening on the set of the Grand Journal. An appointment is made. The next day, Alain Zirah and Mathy Badji went to Le Martinez hotel, accompanied by Lydia Meseguer and Lita CY. Bad news: *Tonight, the set is occupied by Madonna, Sharon Stone, Jean-Claude Van Damme and Jane Birkin...* The team does not dismantle and sends Lita to have the rag dolls signed by Madonna, Sharon Stone, Jean-Claude Van Damme and Jane Birkin... The personalized dolls will be auctioned for UNICEF to benefit sick children during the evening ceremony, sponsored by the Partouche Group.

This Thursday evening, the 3rd edition of the Palmes d'Or des OFF de Cannes 2008 award ceremony took place in the sumptuous setting of the terrace of Hotel 3.14. The purpose of this event is to reward out-of-competition talent at the Cannes Film Festival. This celebration is an original idea of Alain Zirah. Filmmaker and multifaceted artist. He is also president of the Cinq Regards association, whose mission is to support and accompany projects related to cinema. The mistress of ceremony of this beautiful evening, Lydia Meseguer, branding coaching specialist and manager of the operation, was accompanied by mentalist Raymi Phenix. Producers, directors, actors, artists of all kinds were on hand to attend this great evening. Many artists from the Croisette came to complete the animation with clowns, jugglers. Two Charlot doubles will bring their emotions in homage to the 7th art.

OFF DE CANNES 2008 / HOTEL 3.14

HONORARY CHAIRMAN OF THE EVENING: JAN KOUNEN

Jan Kounen is a visionary Franco-Dutch director. His recent films bear witness to his interest in mysticism and forbidden experiences. For Doberman, he introduced Vincent Cassel to Monica Bellucci. Blueberry takes Jean Giraud's cult character, alias Moebius, on an inner adventure via hallucinogenic mushrooms. 99F, based on the novel by Frederic Beigbeder, criticizes the "pensée unique" accentuated by the globalization of ideas. Jan Kounen will select the winners of the OFF de Cannes Palms 2008.

BUT WHO IS AZ?

"From photography to drawing, painting and filmmaking, Alain Zirah is an artist in his own right. As a filmmaker, he offers us a LadyKat on the big screen, a sort of rock Catwoman with a sense of humor and originality. An extroverted jetsetter, he enjoys meeting new people "because every spark of contact with another person triggers a creative inferno". A graphic designer inspired by comics; he creates a multi-chrome virtual world. His confident, professional style is a legacy of his apprenticeship at the Beaux-Arts in Marseille. His abstract expressionist painting takes us down the colorful, creative slopes as much as his computer work. His poems, imbued with romanticism and nostalgia, blend tenderness and imagination... and affirm that God created woman... in his own image. A vagabond of the imagination, he travels the roads of life, from Paris to New York, from Cannes to Los Angeles, from London to Annecy, from Geneva to Monaco... He signs his name AZ, with the tip of his camera." Article by Béatrice Delmont.

A few facets of the enigmatic AZ will be unveiled at the ceremony in a DVD entitled soberly "Who is AZ?", which will be presented on the screens.

HAUTE-COUTURE FASHION SHOW BY MATHY BADJI

Before the awards ceremony, a magnificent and breathtaking catwalk show will be presented by haute-couture stylist Mathy Badji in the salons of the Carlton or on the Martini terrace of the Gray d'Albion. Models from the four corners of the globe will sparkle in silk and beaded lace to the latest music from the Croisette's top DJs. The OFF de Cannes event has contributed to the emergence of new talent.

LADYKAT & THE KAT LADIES

The Kat Ladies are the heroines of a web series. LadyKat is a jetsetter wearing haute-couture gowns and cat masks. She leads the investigation at prestigious parties in search of the serial killer who is terrorizing the jet set. She is accompanied at parties, cocktails and red carpet by mysterious masked women. LadyKat and the Kat Ladies also took part in the opening of Azed's painting exhibition "Acrylic Photographics" at the Eclat de Verre gallery in Marseille, in March 2007.

The Kat Ladies characters were created by Alain Zirah for a web series featuring LadyKat, RoussyKat, DarkieKat, SnowKat and Tigrette. The five characters were made-up by the talented Philippe Podevyne, assisted by Melanie Laurent, and dressed by Mathy Badji, assisted by Alexis Faure. The Kat Ladies adventures were posted on the web at www.dailymotion.com/azed13vip and www.wat.tv/azed13.

To the cheers of the audience and the applause meter, one of the five "Kat Ladies" was to receive an OFF de Cannes Palm. The audience, in a jubilant mood, couldn't decide between the two winners. As a result, Santana aka RoussyKat (5) and Fanny as Tigrette (2) both received an OFF de Cannes 2008 trophy.

The Kat Ladies dressed by Mathy Badji - Make up Philippe Podevyne - Photo: Hugo Mayer

THE KAT LADIES

A cocktail party allowed guests to enjoy the mild May weather around the 3.14 hotel pool, in an enchanting setting opposite the Carlton Intercontinental.

This OFF de Cannes event contributed to the emergence of new talent. It supports UNICEF's charitable activities through the Charity Arts - UNICEF (Special Cannes Festival 2008), with the auction of some Frimousses Dolls signed by Madonna and Sharon Stone, Jean-Claude Van Damme. photos signed by Lady in Renaissance Bubble around the World & the Kat Ladies in 2008 Cannes Festival, works by Artistes Solidaires de l'action *Les Charity Arts* and the Cabriolet Zest of 2008 Generosity Cannes, customized by Lita C.Y. with the support of artists such as Pilu, Ben Vautier, Combas, Wim Delvoye, Pascal Morabito, Moya, Wuis, Michèle Berge, Jean Marc, Teddy...

The theme of the evening was *The Kat Ladies* based on short films shot by Alain Zirah for the web. In this comedy, the masked young women are looking for the serial killer who terrorizes the jet set and the fashion world through terrible crimes.

The presentation of the OFF de Cannes Golden Palms, by the Cinq Regards organization with the participation of Hotel 3.14, as sponsor, brought together many partners, including Def2Shoot, British Films Magazine, Jean Claude Van Damme, Lita CY, Celebrities and Sport Charity; "Les Charity Arts", Olivia Ervi, DMS Debah Sound with DMS Debah Films, Russian Vodka, Hugo Mayer's Blog Reporter, Puyricard chocolate, SL Communication.

The show *The Kat Ladies and the Renaissance Bubble* has put on a musical performance that will be remembered with Lita CY in her bubble surrounded by the five *female Kats* dressed in original outfits by the designer Mathy Badji, assisted by Alexis Faure and made up by Philippe Podevyne and Melanie Laurent.

The 2008 OFF de Cannes Golden Palms awarded some personalities as the French actor Edouard Baer with Yanillys Perez, Simona Graneri, Alain Zirah, Angelique Brando and the famous **Eva Longoria** (Deseperate Housewives) shot with **Bernard Brochand**, the Mayor of Cannes during gala dinner with famous personalities.

The 2008 OFF de Cannes Golden Palms honored the following personalities:

To the acclaim of the professional audience and applause, fashion designer **Mathy Badji** received the 2008 Grand Prix de la mode des OFF de Cannes **Mathy Badji**, as **tomorrow's stylist, for her creativity and her free vision of the Kat Ladies.**

Ruben Arroyo, Spanish comedian, was awarded for his interpretations of Latin lover and graphic artist.

LadyKat, the masked jetsetter, received a trophy for her role as a female cat and her appearances at Cannes parties.

Camille Marty, blog reporter, receives a trophy for her two very complete blogs on cinema www.cinemaniac.fr as well as she completes with www.cinemaniaCannes.fr. **and www. cinemaniacannes.fr**

The actress **Devon Aoki** was at Carlton.

Santana alias RoussyKat and **Fanny** in the role of Tigrette received their OFF de Cannes 2008 trophy sponsored by the partner Franck Malmin for Def2Shoot.

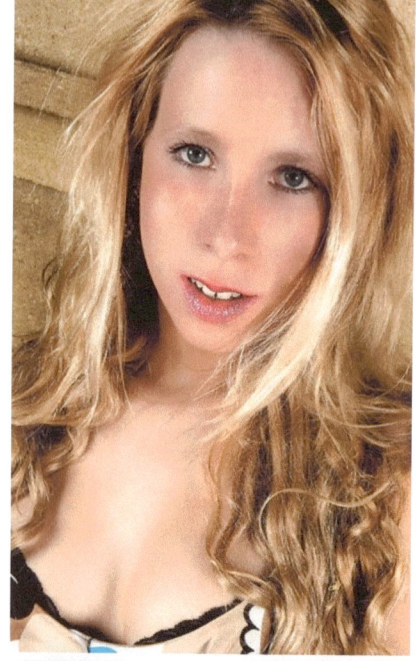

A moment of emotion evokes the memory of the mistress of the 2007 ceremony, the wonderful and always smiling **Fleur Lipp**, who passed away on her 25th birthday, swept away by a devastating illness. She wanted to be in Cannes among us, unfortunately, her forces did not follow her.

Three other talents were also showcased on the hotel 3.14 rooftop: Lesya Matsko, Landryne Agbokpazo and Phoebe Price.

Lesya Matsko, an Ukrainian director graduated from La Femis cinema school, Paris already awarded in Monaco, presents her Slavic charm to the international public of Hotel 3.14, but not for the public around the pool.

Landryne Agbokpazo is a Togolese actress and producer. Selected by a screening, she raised awareness for her fight against malaria in Africa.

Phoebe Price, an American actress from Los Angeles, who won an award as "the diva of the red carpets", could not walk on the purple carpet installed for the occasion by Hotel 3.14.

During the event, we had two photographers, Hugo Mayer and François Maquaire, who captured some moments of memorable evenings with the stars.

Photos : François Maquaire

In Cannes, anything is possible. It was in the toilets of the Eden Roc at the Hôtel du Parc that I met **Jude Law**. We then chatted at length about the film The Astonishing Mr Ripley, a sort of American remake of Plein Soleil starring Alain Delon. It's a pleasant surprise to find myself with Dany Boon and his charming wife, photographed by the camera. I'm on the phone, concentrating hard. A stocky man comes towards me. With a Maori tattoo on half his face. In a soft voice, he indicates that I'm leaning against his car.

Reading on the web, if you're not invited to the Amfar party with **Madonna** and **Sharon Stone**, the best party is on the rooftop of the 3.14 hotel with the OFF de Cannes.

DOLCE & GABBANA PARTY - BAOLI VIP LOUNGE

Record attendance at the Baôli for one of the most prestigious evenings organized by the famous brand, on May 23. As soon as we enter, charming hostesses offer us a pair of black glasses from the Italian brand. We're photographed in front of the photocall alongside some of the world's sexiest actresses, singers and celebrities.

Parisian metro atmosphere at rush hour of chic personalities in tuxedos and beautiful dresses, with a cocktail in hand. My son Pierre-Adrien, 15, was able to get in. For him, it's a real discovery: there are beautiful girls, good music, the alcohol flows freely and you bump into lots of celebrities.

A lost man asks me to take him to the VIP area. It's Tommy Hilfiger. He holds my hand in this festive atmosphere, afraid of getting lost. We meet up with our friend Nicolas Moutte and a host of VIPs, including Valentino, Rose Mc Gowan, Dita von Teese, Naomi Campbell...

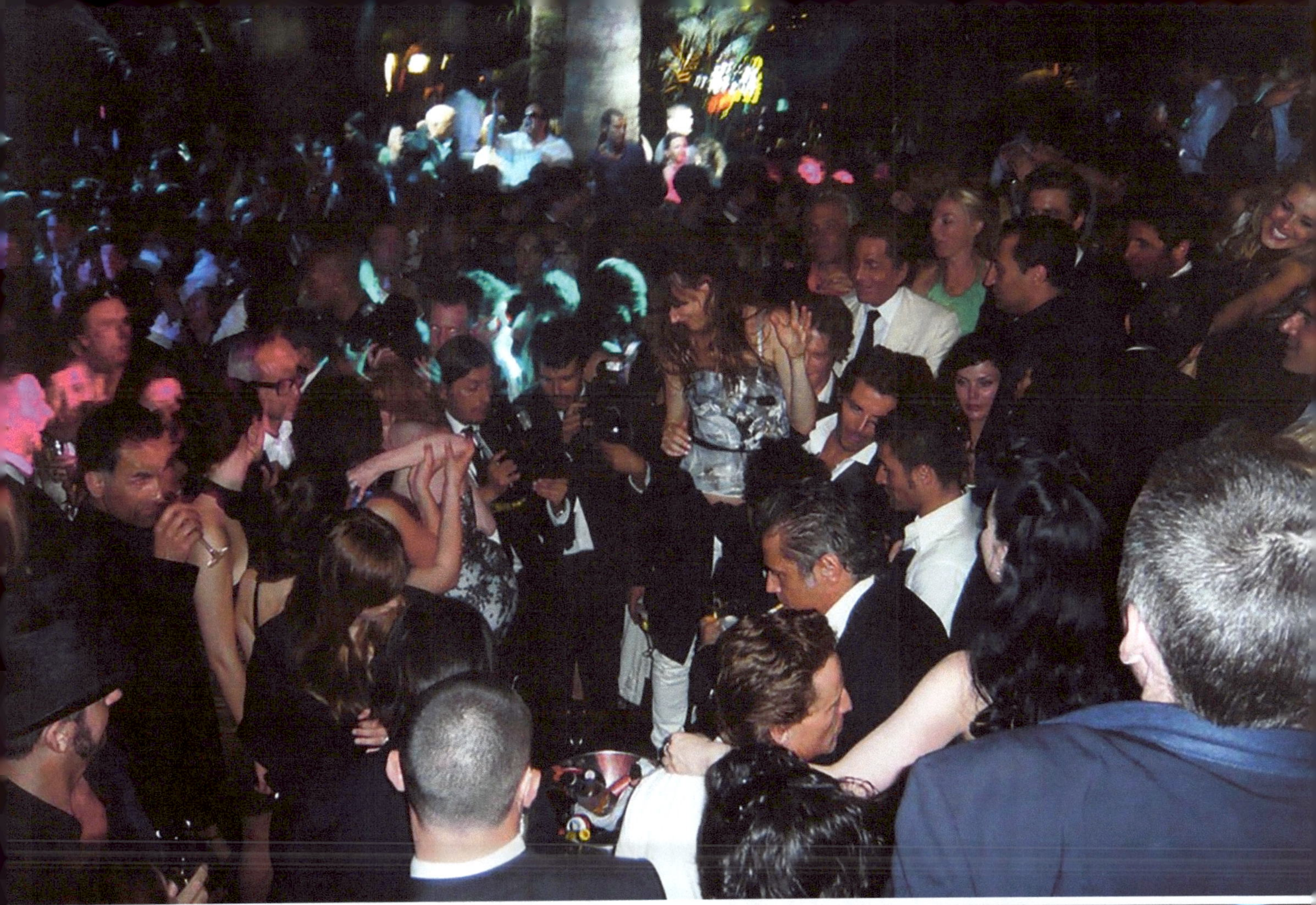

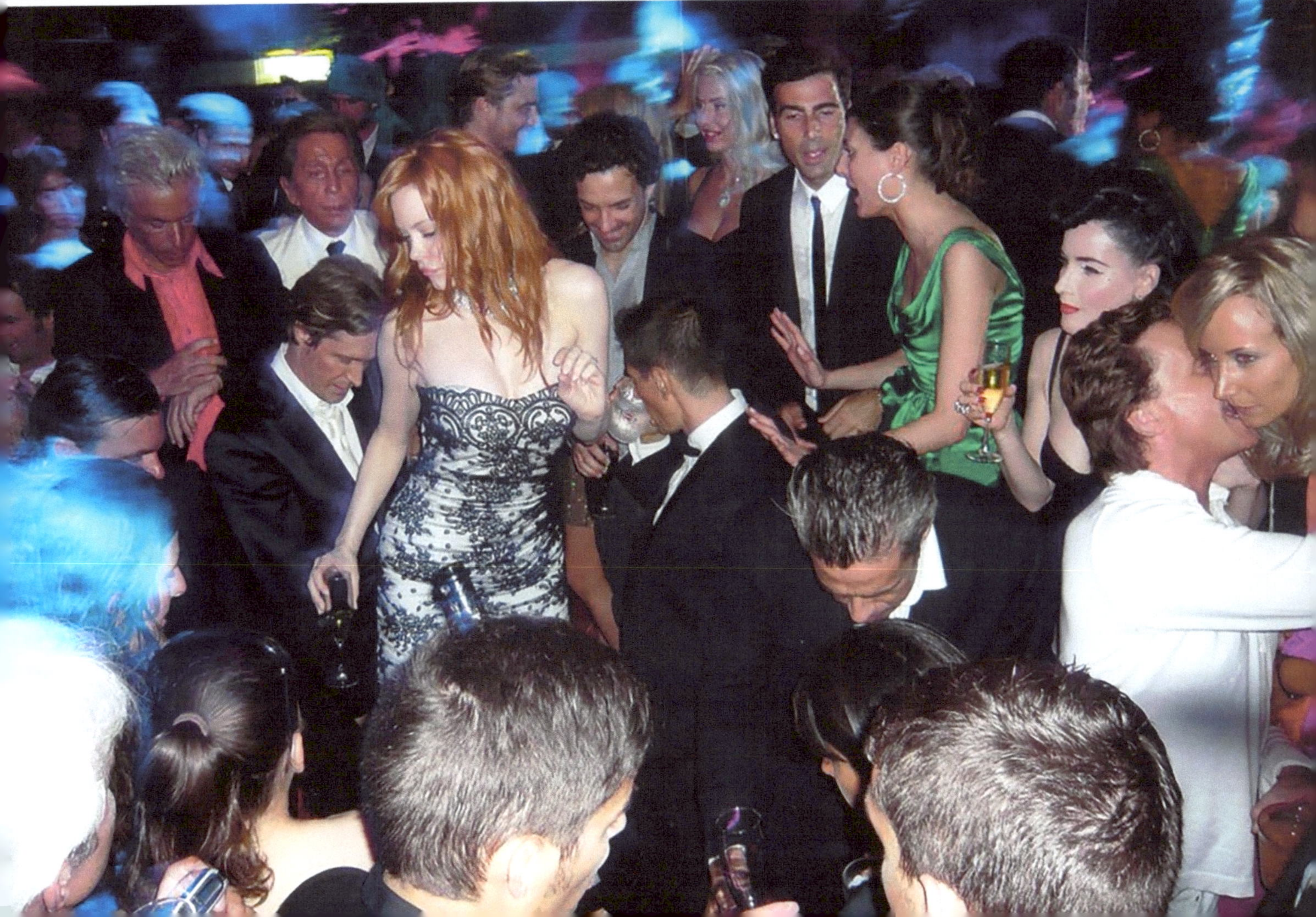

After the OFF de Cannes party, the team goes to Dolce &Gabbana party at Baôli, in a very hot atmosphere, where we meet many famous stars in the VIP area as Dita Von Teese, P. Diddy et Fawaz Gruosi with Naomi Campbell, Rose Mc Gowan and the famous designer Valentino. The party was one of the most famous private parties of Cannes festival. There were so many people, even Tommy Hilfiger had to be helped by OFF de Cannes team to join the VIP area.

Photos : Nicolas Moutte with Mila Jovovic

2009 OFF DE CANNES ON MAJESTIC PONTOON

OFF DE CANNES 2009 - MAJESTIC BEACH

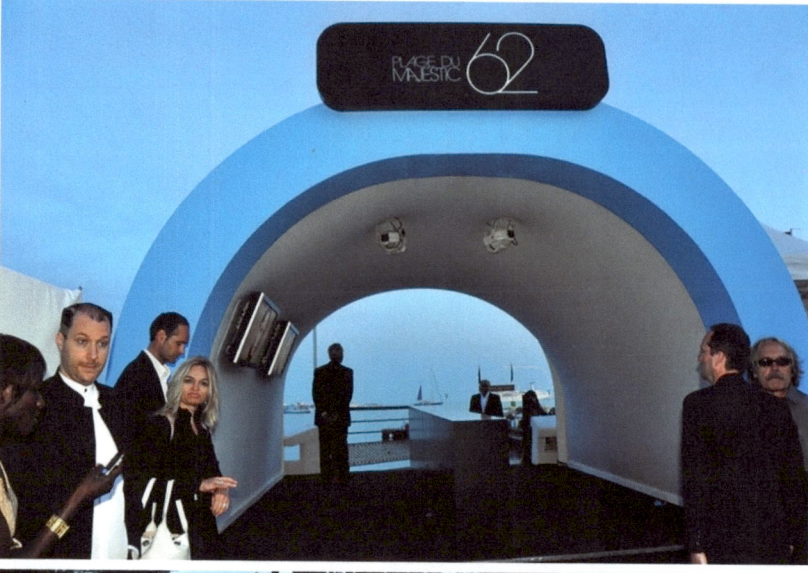

2009, May - After Emir Kusturica and the support of director Jan Kounen, the 2009 OFF de Cannes ceremony was produced under the presidency and with the support of Brazilian writer Paulo Coelho. His latest book, *The Winner stands Alone*, is set in Cannes.

Italian-Argentinian artist Mark-r, who trained at the Colon Theatre in Buenos Aires, created a sculpture of LadyKat, the Kat lady, especially for the 2009 ceremony.

For this iconoclastic ceremony, held on the pontoon of the Majestic beach, after featuring American director Mark W. Gray, blogger Hugo Mayer and his Blogreporter, designer Mathy Badji, actress Phoebe Price and Camille Marty's Cinemaniac blog, an international jury with American directors Mark W. Gray and Steven Kimbrough, Miami-based sound engineer Antoine Lucchetti, and Marseille-based composer Michel Ganteaume. And the winner is...

THE WINNERS OF 2009

The Kat d'Or for music was awarded to Canadian DJ Maurice Eliam aka **DJ Morisson** for his song *I Believe*.

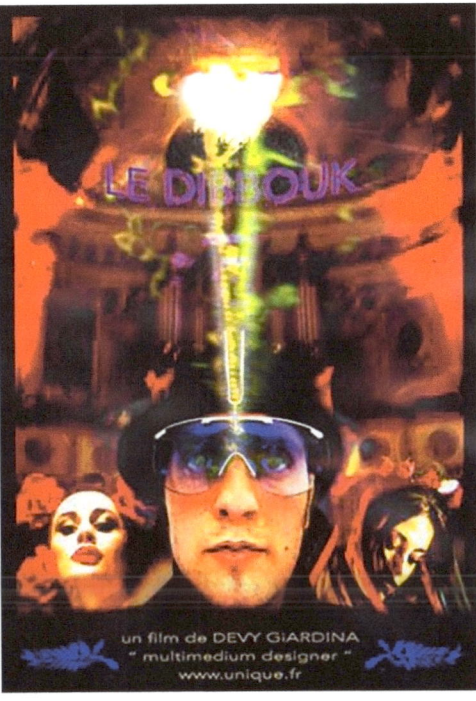

The Kat d'Or for direction went to director and visual and sound designer **Devy Giardina** for his film *The Dibouk*.

The third Kat d'Or spotlighted the multi-talented Los Angeles-based singer and dancer **Michael Brown**, whose catchy music from his latest video, *Please*, has all the makings of a hit if it gets media coverage.

The special Grand Prize of Golden Kat was awarded to mentalist **Raymi Phenix**, an enigmatic character who presented a foretaste show on the road to the bizarre by hypnotizing Mathy Badji in the lobby of the Majestic in front of a stunned audience.

Finally, Alain Zirah presented the 2008 OFF de Cannes Red Carpet Diva Grand Prize rewarded to American actress Phoebe Price, who was unable to receive it the previous year on the terrace of the 3.14 hotel.

The Fashion designer Mathy Badji, who had won the 2008 OFF de Cannes Grand Prize for Fashion introduced one of her creations, worn by Marie Noëlle, a model from Marseilles, Bouches du Rhône departmental council.

A tribute was then paid to Fleur Lipp, the legendary smile. A moving text was read by actress Alexia de Saint John's to pay tribute to the memory of the 2007 Mistress of ceremonies, who passed away too soon at 25, after a travel in Canada. She will always leave a wonderful memory of her passage. All that remained was to thank the guests, partners and sponsors for making this an unforgettable evening, before launching *the Kat Ladies Party* in the mild spring weather of May.

Erik Sebban-Meyer at piano

142

OFF DE CANNES 2010

OFF DE CANNES 2010
CARLTON'S LITTLE BAR

Cannes, 2010, May 20

Five years after the creation of this unique celebration at the heart of the world's biggest event, the jury is gathered around Alain Zirah and his masked creature LadyKat, dazzling in a sparkling yellow dress. Patrick Lachaud, the loyal star presenter of La Locale TV, came to Cannes for the second time to accompany this iconoclastic event.

The contestants will be judged by a jury of professionals presided over by Larry Vickers, dancer and choreographer to Michael Jackson, Tina Turner, Grace Jones and even David Bowie. The jury will spotlight new talent discovered by the team who are in Cannes during the festival. The ceremony will take place three days later, in a secret place. It will only be revealed on the OFF de Cannes Official Group on the eve of May 23rd.
Just another way of keeping the buzz going.

Jury members gather at *Le Carré d'Or.* Larry Vickers and Patrick Lachaud are happy to meet the members. Zachary James Miller is Barack Obama's official representative in France. Don Clovis, Dutch producer of several music bands (Eagles, Fleetwood Mac, Police, Pat Benatar) is also producer for action & martial arts films (Jet Li, Jason Statham). Patrick Murru, set designer for Marco Polo in Beijing, Marquis de Sade at Château Lacoste and costume designer for Pietragalla. Nono *le chat d'gouttière*, is an author and rapper from Seine-Saint-Denis. The American painter, photographer and director Franz Kennedy and French screenwriter Michel Delpigny complete this exceptional jury.

A phone call from Don Clovis tells us that he will unfortunately be absent. He has been in a car accident. In his hospital room, everyone sends him a message wishing him a speedy recovery. The jury gets to know each other and receives information on the competing artists over a friendly drink. After this exchange, the evening continues on the ARTE Yacht, in the company of Hugo Mayer, Michel Rebichon (Premiere Magazine) and Jean-Pierre Lavoignat (Studio Magazine), before continuing at the Terrasse Martini. The evening concludes in the VIP Room with Timbaland and Lionel Richie.

GRACE JONES
LIVE

The day before, it was **Grace Jones'** birthday. Larry Wickers and Alain Zirah offer him a voluminous bouquet of sixty-two white balloons at the Grand Hotel. She loved it. The team meets in the famous secret place. Sometimes divine intervention can work miracles. The team is fortunate to have a two-hour window at Carlton's Little Bar. It is an extremely elitist and private space. Retained from one year to the next.

If the location had been officially announced several days in advance, there would have been a riot. Only about fifty privileged people will have the honor of entering it.

The French photographer **Marie Goujon** receives the OFF de Cannes Grand Prize for Photography for the report she did, along during Grace Jones' birthday.

I m not

paparazzziii

happy birthday
Grace jonns !!

2010 OFF DE CANNES - CARLTON'S LITTLE BAR

Patrick Lachaud, presenter of Locale TV, tried to get information from Larry Vickers about his works with Michael Jackson, Tina Turner, Grace Jones and Moulin Rouge.

Five years after the creation of this unique celebration within the world's largest event. Alain Zirah and his masked creature LadyKat, shot by Marc Lathuilliere, make the show

2010 May, 20

The ceremony will take place three days later, in a still secret place. The members of the jury are gathered in the establishment *Le Carré d'Or/The Golden Square*.

Don Clovis, Dutch producer of several music groups (Eagles, Fleetwood Mac, Police, Pat Benatar) is also producer of some action or martial arts films (Jet Li, Jason Statham).

The members of the jury of the 2010 edition, with as chairman **Larry Vickers**, Michael Jackson's choreographer and coach, as president of the jury. Larry Vickers and Patrick Lachaud are pleased to meet the various members. Zachary James Miller is Barack Obama's official representative in France.

Patrick Murru, scenographer of Marco Polo in Beijing, of the Marquis de Sade at Château Lacoste and costume designer of Pietragalla. **Nono the alley cat**, is an author and rapper from Seine-Saint-Denis. American photographer, painter and director Franz Kennedy and French screenwriter **Michel Delpigny** complete this exceptional jury.

After this exchange, the evening continues, on ARTE Yacht, with Lionelle who began with OFF de Cannes 2007, Hugo Mayer, Michel Rebichon and Jean-Pierre Lavoignat before a party at the Martini Terrace. The evening will end at the VIP Room with **Timbaland** and Lionel Richie.

The arrival of Russian designer **Larisa Katz** with loyal **Tinus D**. shocks everyone. She wears a sculptural white dress topped by an impressive headdress. She is unanimously awarded the OFF de Cannes Grand Prize 2010 for Fashion. The team also honored **Larry Vickers** with a Special Prize for his career as a dancer, choreographer, and for his benevolence.

The Iranian-Brussels singer **Haleh Nasiri** receives a special mention for her trip-hop compositions, including for The Kat Ladies teaser. The jury also gave a special mention to cartoonist **Sophie Janson,** aka Minatsuki Shaolan, who illustrated some of the Kat Ladies characters.

Prior to this, in July, during the Fashion Week in Paris, with the West Indian director Dan Cuquemy, Alain Zirah produced a series of short films with Larisa Kats and her team, entitled *The Aristocratic Punks*. The following year, in Cannes, just before the ceremony, Alain Zirah shot in the streets of the city a slideshow called *2020, Angels of Victory*, which led the designer and her team to head up the three Cannes Festival highlights in the Dutch press.

The privileged few who were able to attend this exceptional event, in the Intercontinental Carlton's Little Bar, had the opportunity to immortalize these moments with the flashes of their cameras. Several selected talents will have the opportunity to take part in a joint the team at the Espace Pierre Cardin in Paris, near Palais de l'Elysee, in October 2011.

The prize-giving ceremony begins with **Sandra Meziere**, who was rewarded for her blog *in the mood for Cannes*. This 7th art lover also announces the upcoming release of three new blogs.

Rosana Golden approves the original and creative universe of **Yaya Moore** and her *Teleportations in a novel* who awarded the OFF de Cannes Grand Prize for Film.

Larisa Katz wears a sculptural white dress topped with an impressive headdress. Unanimously, she was awarded the OFF de Cannes 2010 Grand Prize of Fashion. The **composer Damien Dewulf** wins the 2010 OFF de Cannes Music prize for his setting of poems from Charles Baudelaire's *Flowers of Evil*.

Verane Dombrowski's charm and beauty are rewarded, and she receives the Grand Prize for The Kat Lady of the Year. The Golden Kat. This young actress joins the cast for next shootings, as one of the main actresses of the project of short film *Black Kats*. The actress seduced with several photo shoots.

DarkieKat is the absolute wickedness in the body and face of an angel. She destroys everything she touches. Worse, it can't exist! A challenge for this actress known in the jet set for her charisma and kindness.

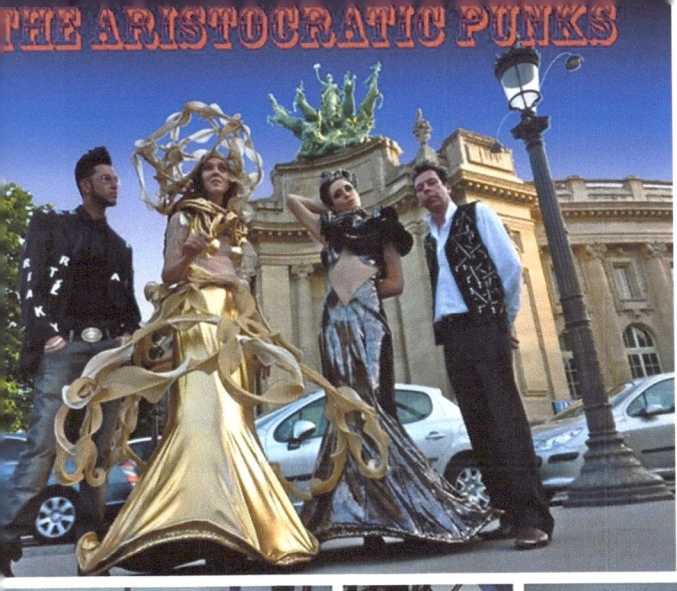

THE ARISTOCRATIC PUNKS

2020 - ANGELS OF VICTORY

LARISA KATZ & FREAKYSTEEL by ALAIN ZIRAH

First French European Indian Fashion Week : Day Two At the Eiffel Tower In Paris
De : Thierry Chesnot
Personnes : Larisa Katz
Afficher images similaires

ZIRAH
ALAIN
DU SANG SUR LE TAPIS ROUGE

KAT LADIES

ART SHOPPING
PARIS · CARROUSEL DU LOUVRE

After making short films in 2010 and 2011, Alain Zirah and Anne Gomis helped the winning designer organize her fashion show on the second floor of the Eiffel Tower (a first) in October 2016. They meet again at the Carrousel du Louvre for the release of the book Du Sang sur le Tapis Rouge (Editions Thierry Sajat).

ALAIN ZIRAH & ANNE GOMIS

2011 FRANCE 3 – FRENCH TV SHOW

Sitting next to Alain Zirah, the mayor of Cannes, Bernard Brochand, helps the presentation of Carolien ter Linden and his book during the TV show *Midi en France* on France 3, hosted by Laurent Boyer and Frédéric Soulié. Then the team gathered for the Jackson Party, with a presentation of the *Glitter & Glam* book by Alain, dressed by Tinus D. Freakystyle in front of Jackson car. Alain and Anne take the pose at VIP Room.

OFF DE CANNES 2011 - JURY MEMBERS

The ceremony is an opportunity to discover and reward the Talents of tomorrow, through a competition on the Web. The members of the jury for 2011 are hosted by **Richard Nilsson**, founder of Residence Superieur and owner of Villa Oxygene, where he welcomes the members of the jury and the various winners.

Afida Turner, singer, songwriter famous for her buzz, has shared her life between France and the United States for 12 years, as Tina Turner's daughter in law. Woman with a big heart, she supports new talents in her last album called Paris-Hollywood.

Larisa Katz, winner of the Grand Prize of Fashion at OFF de Cannes 2010, designer of Russian origin living in Holland. Last year, she presented her new collection at Mercedes' 125th anniversary celebration in Maastricht. A great discovery by OFF de Cannes 2010.

Zachary James Miller is a man of many facets: behind his hat as a producer and director of documentaries and TV series lies a distinguished doctorate in psychology, as well as Vice-President of the American Democratic Party in France. He actively campaigned for Barack Obama in the 2008 presidential elections. He officially represents President Barack Obama in France.

Judi Beecher is an internationally renowned American actress, producer and singer. From her beginnings in New York theaters to the production of films such as "*Only in Paris*" and "*Finding Isabelle*", not to mention her singing career, she has constantly added to her many talents. Having appeared in the blockbusters "*Armageddon*" and "*Stepford Wives*", Judi has also starred in hit series such as "*The Shield*" and "*New York: Cops*". She also played the lead character in Sony's "Heavy Rain" video game. She has just finished shooting Salvatore Sorentino's feature film "*The Warrior and the Savior*" in New York.

Judith Freiha is an American actress, model for fashion, but also furniture designer. She is also a jack-of-all-trades. From comedy (Press *Conference* by Matthieu Mai 1st Audience Award at the World AIDS Conference in Vienna 2010. *The Inseparables* by Fabrice Bracq) to furniture design and fashion, this Paris-based American also works in production. Aleksandra Bosnjak's docu-drama *Road to Love* (UK Production) is her latest feature film.

Photo Franz Fox Kennedy

OFF DE CANNES
CEREMONY 2011
6 ème édition
En partenariat avec
MISS @FRICA UNITED
la soirée de pré-lancement

Tinus D. Freakysteel, Dutch artist, designer of steel, has worked with the designer on various projects, for which he made accessories. This master of steel, his material of choice. Far from its usual use, he doesn't confine himself to design. He transforms iron into luxury garments, bags and various art pieces.

Eugene Mandelcorn, an American producer, is a talent scout. He works with 25 directors preparing their first feature film, for which he seeks financing through crowd funding.

Michael Errington, a Franco-British composer, film music producer and complete musician, received an award at Hampton's Film Festival and a Gold Award at the World Fest Houston International Film Festival. The German national ZDF broadcast him for a live concert from a large hall in Munich.

Jordi Casals is a French painter and gallery owner in Monaco, passionate about Salvador Dali to whom he has devoted several exhibitions and books. Tonight, he presents the Michael Jackson hyper realistic statue made with silicone.

Anacole Daalderop is a Franco-Dutch composer and multi-instrumentalist from the Paris Conservatory. He has created eclectic music albums including *"Metaluminium"* within his company Live Again Production. He composed film soundtracks as well as productions with other artists, each time with a highly 80s-inspired touch. Keen to share his experience, Anacole teaches History of Art and Music, and gives audio technique courses geared towards song production.

Thanks to the public relations work done by Beatrice Touitou and Linda Cohen, the presentation will take place at Hôtel Embassy. Jordi Casals and Adrien Saada did us the great honor of presenting the hyper-realistic silicone statue of Michael Jackson on May 17 and 18. She will follow us from Hotel Embassy to Villa Oxygene. Thus, the honorary president of the OFF de Cannes 2011 is a virtual Michael Jackson. A great moment will be the meeting where Joseph Jackson will find himself face to face with the statue of his son. Then, the statue is installed in an excalibur alongside Afida Turner for a tour of the Croisette that will surprise many.

After the evening of May 17 at the Atrium Beach Croisette, in partnership with Miss Africa United and Tendance TV, the films were screened in front of a large audience in the salons of the Embassy Hotel on May 18. Jury members took note of their favorites. The winners were announced in the presence of Richard Nilsson, during the pool evening at the Villa Oxygène. The OFF de Cannes organized the first fashion show for young designer Fahaid Sanober, followed by the presentation of 7 trophies to the winners of 2011.

OFF DE CANNES 2011 - 2014

THE GREAT INTERNATIONAL WEB FILM COMPETITION

The OFF de Cannes Ceremony is a good opportunity to discover and reward tomorrow's web talent, through the competition created by Anne Gomis. The theme for 2011 was: "**Children born in 2000 will be twenty in 2020**".

The pre-launch party took place on May 17 at Atrium Beach La Croisette, in partnership with Miss Africa United and Tendance TV. Then, the 3-minute digital films were screened in front of a packed audience in the lounges of the Hotel Embassy, on May 18. Jury members under the presidence of Max Howard (Disney) took good notes of their favorites. The results of the votes were announced in the presence of Richard Nilsson, patron of the event, at the trophy ceremony held by the poolside of the Villa Oxygene, during the evening.

7 trophies were awarded to the candidates Winners of the OFF de CANNES 2011 who enter the FACTORY and are:

The gothic filmmaker **Morgan Priest** received the Grand Prize for his 3-minute film «*Kannibale*» which could become the pilot for digital series.

Prize of Animation 3D: **Vanessa Veillé** and the **INTERFACTORY** team received the Prize for *Bébé Lily/The adventures of Baby Lily, the musical*..

The jury chose two ex-aequo artists in very different styles for the Prize of Music with the French rock band **IZUL,** (photography) for the clip "I Wonder" and **Philippe from JB's** for the clip *"Ce soir ou Jamais/ Tonight or Never"*.

Grand Prize of Fine Arts: **Franck Katz** received the prize for his rotating painting and his video about the Subtle Art called *L'Art Subtil* – The OFF de Cannes producers gave him the opportunity to show his Art to the jackson Family Foundation.

Prize of Fashion: **Soso** for the originality and multicolored Art Style video clip *Sista Sila*.

Grand Prize of Photography: **Jon Cafee** received and Awards for the photo direction of his video clip: *Homo Gene*.

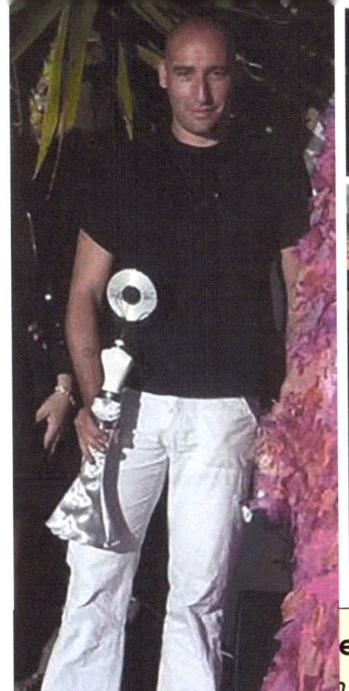

...eve Favouille** from Marseilles received the Special Prize for Digital Film *...n of the card game* » by Marcel Pagnol.

Special Mention goes to Norwegian photographer **Charles Lloyd Williams** for the quality and originality of his photos presented in «My Work» by Acestudio.

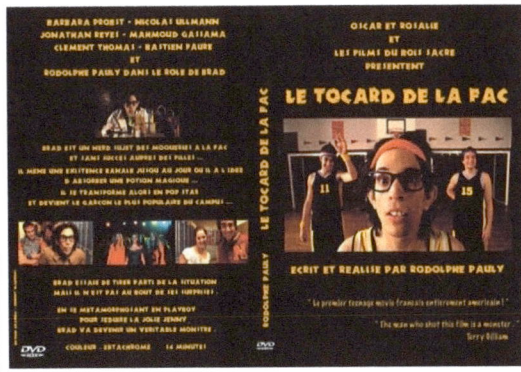

The young director **Rodolphe Pauly** received an encouragement for the originality of his short film *Welcome to Cannes*. A special mention also goes to director **Costas Kostaris** for his film: «Le Nuage» (The Cloud), whose teaser for the feature film is out of category.

After the ceremony, the Winners gather around the VILLA OXYGENE swimming pool for a wild evening, until the wee hours.

The following day, the Winners are invited to the Majestic, partner of the OFF de Cannes, for Fashion TV's Most Liked Models Awards.

Then screening of the digital films took place in front of a large audience in the lounges of Hôtel Embassy, on May 18. The members of the jury had the screening of the three-minute short films dedicated to a large audience in the lounges of the Hôtel. The members of the jury took time to pose for medias.

A special mention of encouragement is also given to the young director **Rodolphe Pauly** for the originality of his film *Bienvenue à Cannes/Welcome to Cannes* presented out of competition.

The team goes the day after to the *F*ck me I'm Famous* show by Cathy and her husband **David Guetta**.

THE MEANING OF LIFE

In 2011, Alain is invited with his little sister at heart, Angelique Brando, Marlon Brando's daughter, to a cocktail party hosted by the mogul Harvey Weinstein, one of the most famous American producers with Miramax. The private cocktail was organized at the Gray d'Albion penthouse. Only about eighty major American producers were present, including **Max Howard**, producer of The *Lion King* for Disney. He launched the animation film *Igor*. The following year, Max called Alain to tell him that he wanted to join the jury for the OFF de Cannes. Of course, with such a background, he was chosen to become the jury president for 2012. In company of partner **Bruno Chatelin**, Filmfestivals.com, Anne Gomis was an excellent hostess for him and Doy Dalling. In fact, Max asked to extend his mandate for another year. He was the only one for two years running. For 2013, he will come with his partner Jay Shindell.

The OFF de Cannes Festival presents TOMORROW'S TALENTS (2012-2020). The 2012 OFF de Cannes Digital Film Grand Competition will take place from February 1 to May 20, 2012, around the central theme "**The Meaning of Life**". Created in Cannes in 2005, the OFF de Cannes ceremony is an opportunity to discover and reward the talents of tomorrow, present on the Web through a competition.

Candidates working in the creative professions that revolve around image, music and fashion as well as amateur artists will have to imagine the artistic sensitivity. They will go to best use our five senses (sight, hearing, smell, taste, touch).

The team reinforced by Anne Gomis invites artists to participate in the 2012 digital film competition. We hope to discover, among the candidates, the future greats of the Cannes Film Festival. It's about illustrating in a three-minute film because you will be one of the talents of 2020.

Each film selected will still have to have meaning in 2020. Do not hesitate to propose us some avant-garde films, using all the new technologies at your disposal (3D, relief, olfactory films, audio-description, subtitles, augmented reality...) to make the public discover how far the technology can go.

The OFF de Cannes complement the Cannes International Film Festival, because today, cinema is caught up or even surpassed by television, laptops and smartphones...

We are convinced that tomorrow talents are being expressed today with digital cameras and smartphones to create videos that they can broadcast.

At this revolutionary time, the Web plays an essential role in the instantaneous and globalized diffusion of images.

The OFF de Cannes website is equal to the ambitions of the artists represented in La Factory, on which participants, media or fans will be able to access all their documents and information online.

Les "Off de Cannes" made in Marseille

Depuis 2005, Alain Zirah, dit Azed, et Solène Guionnet, dite Ladykat, organisent en marge du Festival international du film, leurs "Off de Cannes." Loin de vouloir supplanter le festival, les "Off" aspirent à le compléter en mettant à l'honneur les nouveaux talents du web.

Tournés vers les nouvelles technologies et moyens de communication, les "Off" récompensent chaque année des artistes dans sept catégories. *"Les talents de demain sont sur le web et filment avec des caméras numériques ou des Smartphones!"*, commente Azed. Ces nouveaux talents sont ainsi mis à l'honneur le temps, au moins, du festival. Et pour la 6ᵉ édition, le traditionnel concours du film numérique de 3 minutes est placé sous le thème "2020 tous reporters, tous cinéastes".

Pour coller à l'ambiance du Festival de Cannes, qui se dé-

roulera du 11 au 22 mai, les "Off" ont prévu notamment une cérémonie de remise des prix, *"dans un lieu prestigieux secret"* de la Croisette. Ouverte au public, la cérémonie aura lieu le 18 mai après délibération du jury. Elle sera animée par Ladykat, vêtue, comme chaque année, de son costume de la déesse égyptienne Bastet, protectrice des artistes.

Mais si les "Off de Cannes" se voient déjà exportés à l'étranger, en Russie ou en Tunisie, ils n'oublient pas d'où ils viennent pour autant. *"Les Off de Cannes sont organisés par des Marseillais,* poursuit Azed. *Et on aimerait vraiment récompenser davantage d'artistes marseillais ou de la région."*

À bon entendeur... Marseillais, à vos smartphones !

M.S.

Inscriptions closes le 15 mai 2011
Informations : www.off-de-cannes.com

Hier, l'équipe des "Off de Cannes" présentait son festival à l'Espace Écureuil, rue Montgrand. / PHOTO M.S.

Espace Écureuil

Press conference at Squirrel Space

A press conference is organized with the support of the Caisse d'Epargne bank of Marseilles, represented by Paule Touitou, on the initiative of Beatrice Touitou and Linda Cohen, and the City of Marseille, represented by Orlando Carvalho. For the first time, the City of Marseille officially recognizes the activities of Alain Zirah, Solene Guionnet and Anne Gomis and supports the OFF de Cannes. Beatrice Touitou and Linda Cohen were particularly efficient in organizing this event in one of Marseille's cultural venues promoted by the Caisse d'Épargne, represented here by Paule Touitou, Head of Communications. After some articles in foreign countries, La Provence newspaper talks about the event.

OFF DE CANNES 2012 - JURY MEMBERS

There was no godfather in 2012, but two godmothers: Her Royal Highness Esther Kamatari and Hermine de Clermont-Tonnerre :

Her Royal Highness Esther Kamatari, OFF de Cannes godmother:

Esther Kamatari is a model, royal highness, politician and writer. She's a grande dame. An exiled Burundian princess in Paris, she turned to fashion, becoming the first black French model and muse of the Jean-Luc François label. Also known for her humanitarian missions to victims of Burundi's civil war, she founded the Abahuza party and entered politics. In 2005, she ran for president of Burundi. As municipal councillor in Boulogne-Billancourt since 2008, with responsibility for international solidarity, she is a woman with an impressive career.

Princess Hermine de Clermont-Tonnerre - 2nd OFF de Cannes godmother

Hermine De Clermont-Tonnerre is the heiress of an illustrious family. Hermine became a designer with Dior at the age of twenty-two. Queen of the jet set, Hermine now runs her own communications agency. As passionate writer, in 1996 she successfully published *Politeness obliges* and other works such as *One day my prince will come*. Several other books were published between 2001 and 2009 by Jean-Claude Lattès. Although unable to attend Cannes, Hermine de Clermont-Tonnerre is a sponsor of our events.

Max HOWARD, Chairman of the Jury :

Max Howard is a British film producer and actor based in Los Angeles. His credits include films such as *Who Framed Roger Rabbit ?* , *Stallion of the Cimarron* and *Igor*. Executive Producer for *Spirit* at DreamWorks. Executive Producer for *The Lion King*... Mr. Max Howard also set up the Disney studio in Paris. Throughout his animation career, Max Howard has worked with UNICEF to bring social messages to developing countries...

Bruno Gaccio, leader of *Les Guignols de l'Info*, writes the lines for the famous latex puppets, alongside Lionel Dutemple, Ahmed Hamidi and Julien Hervé. Between 1998 and 1999, he also presented Un an de plus, before handing over to Laurent Ruquier. With José Garcia, he took part in Philippe Gildas's "Nulle Part Ailleurs" show. Producer, humorist and director, he created the puppet musical Avenue Q de Broadway, which played at the Bobino theater.

Composer, producer and musician **Alan Reeves** has a career studded with prestigious awards for his musical creations, including 35 Academy Awards. A pianist of genius, he has accompanied such greats as The Beatles, The Who, Prince, The Rolling Stones, The Animals, Rod Stewart, Chuck Berry, Lionel Ritchie, Gene Vincent, Murray Head, Serge Gainsbourg, Charles Aznavour, Nino Ferrer, Alain Souchon, Dalida, Chaka Kahn, Otis Redding, Jimi Hendrix, Eric Clapton, Wilson Picket... He has also composed the soundtrack for Cannes 2001 Award-winner *Parle avec les Lions*, IMAX's *Ocean Oasis* and Quentin Tarantino's *Kill Bill 2*...

Zachary James Miller is Barack Obama's personal representative in France. American-born and based in Paris, he is also a producer and director of documentaries, TV series and films, as well as a parapsychologist, counselor, therapist and educator of students of the paranormal & occult. His lecture on consciousness, intention, belief and emotion is an insight into the subject matter of his lectures around the world. He has supported the OFF de Cannes since 2009. He appears in the first book of Alain Zirah called *Strass & Paillettes/ Glitter & Glam* about a festival-goer's diary of 2010 Cannes Film Festival.

Aissatou Thiam made her film debut in 1993 alongside Vincent Lindon. An incredible career for this Senegalese beauty, author of the book *A great laugh*.. Ariel Zeitoun, Claude Lelouch and Luc Besson would certainly say of Aissatou Thiam that she had all the makings of a budding film star, hence her encounters with Robert de Niro and Denzel Washington. She plays in the series *Tropiques Amers/ Bitter Tropics.*

Larisa Katz, born in 1974 in the former Soviet Union, lives in the Netherlands. She has always been passionate about art and the wonders of the world. As fashion designer, she creates sculptural haute couture dresses and headpieces with an Orthodox influence, combining visions of Eastern and Western cultures. Playing with different materials and shapes, she creates timeless, romantic dresses that resemble sculptures, and made a name for herself in Cannes in 2010, where she was awarded the OFF de Cannes Grand Prize of Fashion. Over the past two years Larisa has shown her designs from Amsterdam to Dubai, from Bahrain to London, from NYC to Berlin. Since 2011, she has been a OFF de Cannes jury member, dressing Dita von Teese and made a catwalk for former president Mikhaïl Gorbatchev.

Tinus D. Freakysteel is a Dutch artist, designer and sculptor, working with steel to create fashion accessories (handbags and luminous masks, crowns, chainmail jackets...). Born in 1969, his first major exhibition in 1997, *Trash or Treasure*, got him noticed, and in 2009 he opened his FREAKY STEEL studio in Hoorn with the Wastelanders troupe, a clever blend of Middle Ages and steampunk. As Larisa Katz partner, Tinus D. has been discovered by OFF de Cannes since 2010, and has been a member of the jury since 2011.

Selina De Maeyer is a young Belgian photographer who took up photography in 2008 after studying at Saint Lucas University in Brussels. Born into a creative family, she has drawn, sculpted and painted extensively. But photography allows her to develop emotions, aesthetics and a very personal atmosphere. She retouches all her photos to give them that special atmosphere. The softness of the subjects in a natural setting that has become extraordinary. As partner of Larisa Katz and Tinus D. Freakysteel, she became the youngest OFF de Cannes member of the 2012 jury.

Kris Benard is an actor working in dubbing. Since 2009, he has also been in charge of dubbing for fiction and animation in all formats, and artistic director at CQFD dubbingpictures. After doing the voices in *The Engulfed Worlds* 1985-87 and *Rayman* in 1995, he played in *Go to Hell* in 2000. More recently, he dubbed the voices in the animated series *Batman La Relève/Batman beyond* and dubbed the foreign versions of Luc Besson's feature *The Extraordinary Adventures of Adèle Blanc-Sec*.

Bernard Ramel, specializing in Afro-American black music. With Black Diamond Events, he has produced public shows and private showcases with major international stars such as Salif Keita, Youssou N'Dour, Thione Seck, Alan Reeves, Kool & The Gang and Billy Paul. He is planning a Chuck Berry farewell concert in Europe and a show with the historic musicians of this founder of Rock'n'roll.

Guillaume Ivernel, cartoonist, computer graphics artist and animator. After training at the Dupperey school, he directed commercials with Jean-Pierre Jeunet, and pilots for Gaumont, Xilam and Sparx. Guillaume Ivernel also worked on the storyboard for Starwatcher, a film by Moebius. In 2008, with Arthur Qwak, he directed his animated hit Chasseurs de dragons. Guillaume Ivernel is currently working on a feature-length animated film entitled Soul Man. Unable to attend Cannes, he nevertheless supports the OFF de Cannes team.

Photo Franz Fox Kennedy

IN THE FAMOUS FRENCH MAGAZINE L'EXPRESS

L'EXPRESS

THE OFF DE CANNES IN SEARCH OF TOMORROW'S TALENT.

"Every year for the past 7 years, the OFF de Cannes has rewarded the "talents of tomorrow" through a competition, which for this edition will have as its theme "The Meaning of Life". The winner will be announced on May 18. Founded by Alain Zirah, who was joined by Anne Gomis, the OFF de Cannes are a kind of antechamber to the big Cannes Festival, complementing it with parallel programming. The OFF de Cannes develop an underground culture that doesn't fit into the selection criteria of the festival and its short film corner. In search of avant-garde talent and projects, OFF de Cannes' manager Anne Gomis aims to give a voice to the artists who will give meaning to art in 2020. To enter, candidates must adhere to a 3-minute video format in one of seven categories of their choice - fiction, acting, fashion, dance, visual arts, comedy, music video. With a wide range of tools at their disposal, candidates must respect the theme of the "Senses of Life" (hearing, smell, touch, sight, taste). The jury is chaired by Max Howard, an animation specialist who has worked on films such as *The Little Mermaid* and *The Lion King*".

Photo Franz Fox kenne

Photo Franz Fox Kenne

OFF DE CANNES 2012
ATRIUM BEACH & CARLTON BEACH

The Great Contest of Numeric film on the Web features seven categories. It is organized on the OFF de Cannes official website and the Facebook Groupe Les OFF de Cannes. Professionals are invited to attend the presentation of artists evening on May 22, first at the Atrium Beach, then the screening at Les Arcades theater, and finally, the following day, the awards ceremony on May 23, at Carlton Beach. During these events, Alain and Anne introduced to the public the following Fashion show and musical show case with many artists:

- **Fahaid Sanober**, a young fashion designer (18) and his team, Jennifer and Hermine, put on his second fashion show. The OFF de Cannes gave him the opportunity to create his 1st fashion show for the 2011 OFF de Cannes ceremony at the Villa Oxygene, during the Jackson Party.
- **Kennie Quest**, singer, after presenting her 2011 ceremony at Villa Oxygène, OFF de Cannes presents her Tribute to James Bond show, with Sean Connery lookalike Francesco.

- The colombian swimwear show by **PHAX**.
- **Larisa Katz** (discovered at Off de Cannes 2010, and now a reference in the fashion world), Tinus d. Freakysteel and Selina de Maeyer do their new fashion show with a dress lit by LEDs.
- **Ron Lloyd** (vocals + dance) with his dancers.
- **Alex Alistair**, singer-songwriter (a discovery by Alain Zirah and Anne Gomis).

The songwriter and singer **Alex Alister** was proud to encounter Bruno Gaccio and made a greay show case about the songs from his last album that he introduces in Musicatheme talkshow at Radio JM Marseilles.

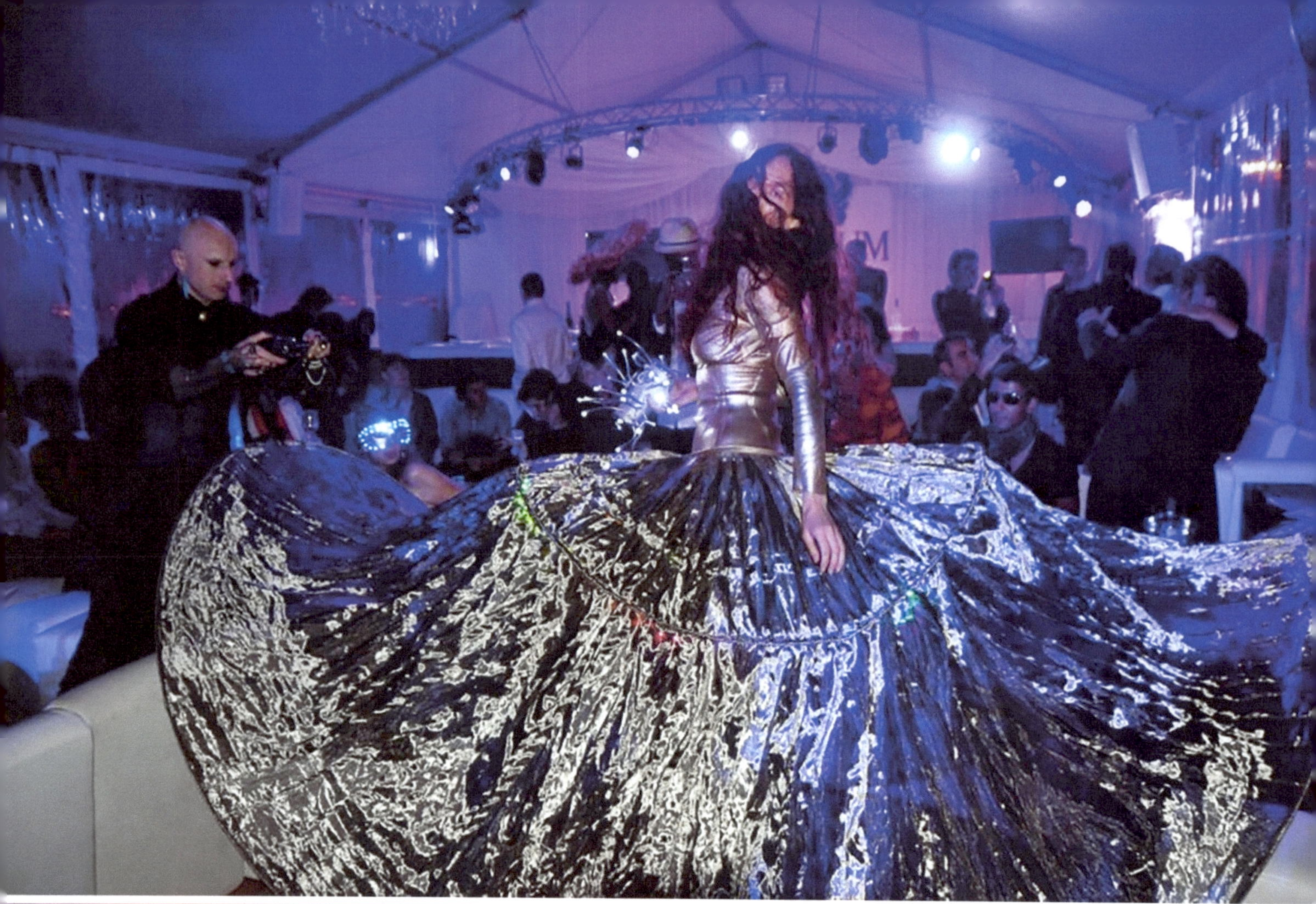

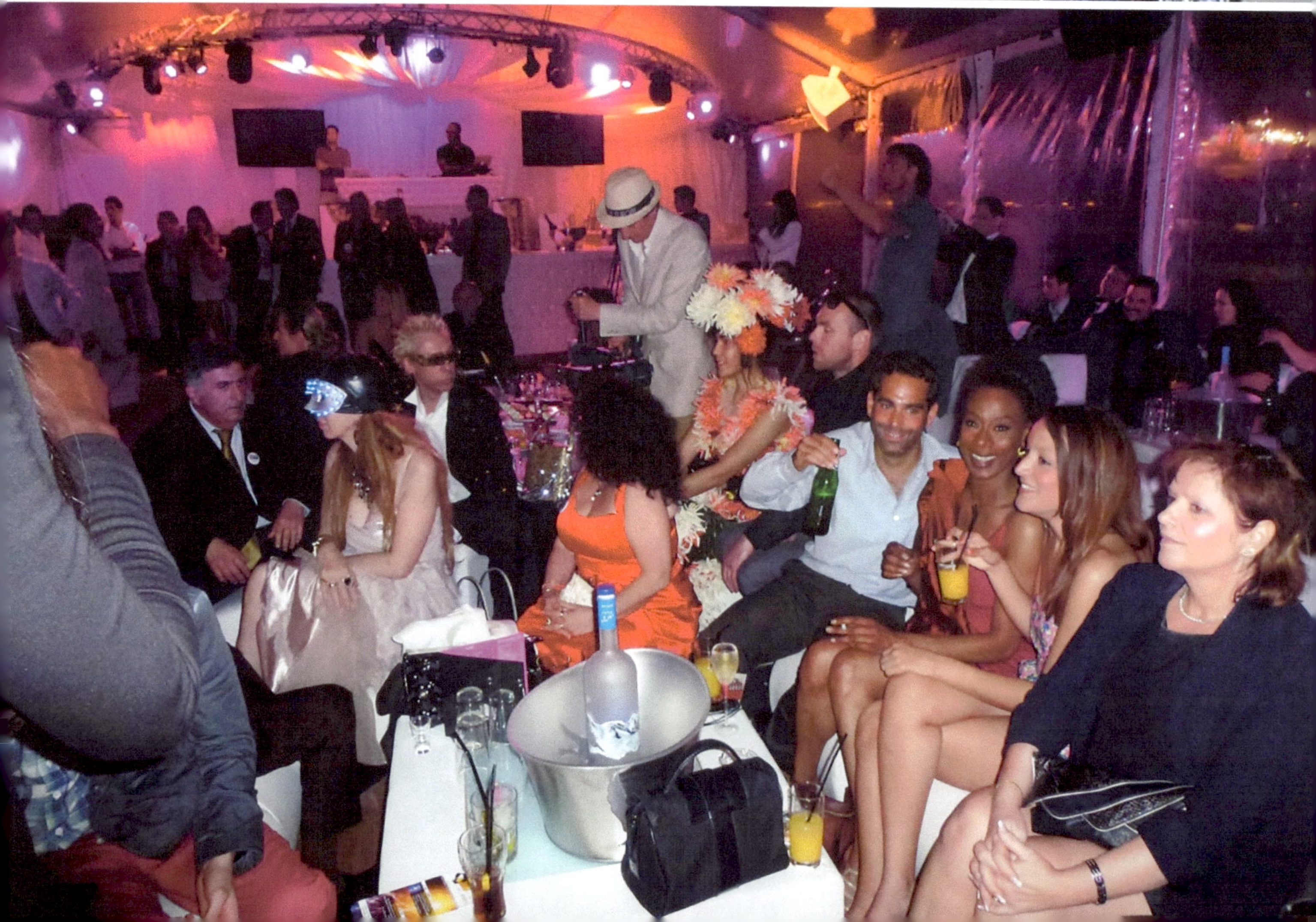

OFF DE CANNES 2012 WINNERS

Following screenings of the shortlisted films at Les Arcades cinema and then at Carlton Beach, the 2012 OFF de Cannes awards ceremony took place on Carlton beach, presided over by Max Howard, Disney producer of *The Lion King*.

The 2012 winners are:
- best actor: **Jicey Carina** for his role in the film *The Unfortunate Chance to Meet* by Charly MG.
- Best Actress: **Mari Yoshida**, from Tokyo, Japan, in the film *The Blood* by Guillaume Tauveron.
- Best Performance: **Raphaël Mouradian** in *Lovers Quiproquo* by Damien Dupuis.
- Best Director: **Pascal Gontier** for the film *A Little Lesson in Good Manners*, starring Bernard Menez and Chris Egloff.
- Best music: **Anacole Daalderop** received the OFF de Cannes 2012 Grand Prize of Music for his album *Black Aluminium*.
- Best adaptation of the theme the meaning of life: **Réjane Avazeri** for her film *Cliché*.

Photo Franz Fox Kennedy

- Favorite: *Nosce Te Ipsum* (know thyself), best director: **Réjane Ruby**; best actor: **Thierry Lemoine**.

Alain Zirah and Anne Gomis were delighted to introduce guests at Les Arcades theater two great Russian artists discovered by their partner Stella Art International:

- **Irina Alaverdova** from Moscow for her nostalgic pastels on Marilyn Monroe. & **Alexey Chirkov** from St Petersburg for his impressive mosaic portraits of Bonaparte to Nanni Moretti, president of the 2012 Cannes Film Festival jury.

 - a special Grand Prize for painting at Cannes 2012 is awarded to mosaic artist Alexey Chirkov from Saint-Petersburg (fine arts category) ex æquo with Irina Alaverdova from Moscow (painting category) with our congratulations to Stella Kalinina for her beautiful fashion and painting presentation with the singer The Voice, on 2012, May 17 at the Yacht-Club.

The award of the Grand Prix OFF de Cannes Film Festival to artist Alexei Chirkov was shown on Russian TV show for a portrait in the technique of the pictorial mosaic "Chevalier de la palme d'or", 2012. The event was organized jointly with the French Association for the Support of the Stella Art International with participation in the cultural program of the Cannes Film Festival. The singer Alex Alister takes the pose with the Russian winners.

The event's producers take this opportunity to thank their partners Emmanuelle Herard (champagne bulles de jazz), Microsoft, Msn.Fr, Filmfestivals, Bruno Chatelin, Radiostar, IEJ (Institut Européen de Journalisme), Pape Diouf, Jean-Pierre Foucault, Nathalie Paoli, Loïse-Isabelle Delassus, Virginie Huleux, Tony Piro, Mariem Coline Tabita, who designed the Cannes OFF trophies for Esbam (Marseille School of Fine Arts).

"Many thanks to all the members of the OFF de Cannes 2012 team: Christian Carniel, Lydia Meseguer, Imane Bess, Romain Lebeau, Sébastien Kocet, Guillaume Gomis, Océane, A Kessy as well as Mary De Vivo (Le Réservoir - Paris) and Smoothbox. Thanks to our official photographers: Alex de Rochant, Franz Fox Kennedy and Romain Duval for their involvement and efficiency, and to our loyal presenter Patrick Lachaud from La Locale TV.

Thanks to our **media partners** who supported or followed the OFF de Cannes events:

L'Express, Canal+, Direct star, La Locale TV, Le Figaro, France 3, LCM, Tendance TV, Msn.fr, Var-Matin, L'Hebdo de Marseille, France Inter, Radio Star, Filmfestivals. com, Le Blogreporter, Cinemaniac & Cinemaniacannes, Maje Officiel, radio RJM, Radio Galère, Radio Dialogue... as well as Libération, La Provence, La Marseillaise, Le Mague.net, Les Inrockuptibles, Marseille Le Jour & La Nuit, Metro, ANBTV, British Film and for our fashion discoveries: Fashion TV, RTL Germany, L1TV, TVL, Elle, Gala, Madame Figaro, Vogue, Glamour, etc.".

Photo Franz Fox Kennedy

OFF DE CANNES 2013 AT EDEN

May 21, 2013. The project.

Since 2005, the OFF de Cannes have been making a lasting impact by setting themselves apart in the service of talent. "We showcase talent that isn't in the official selection because it's too avant-garde or doesn't fit into the categories in the running," explains Alain Zirah, co-producer with Anne Gomis. Rewarded disciplines: cinema, fiction, fashion, music, visual arts and photography... «everything that revolves around cinema».

The OFFs started from a single observation: "It's difficult for artists to make films. So the idea was to help talented people with their projects, and to put the spotlight on them, with the Cannes Film Festival acting as a sounding board. He underlines: "Since the new generation of artists is breaking the codes of the cinematographic arts, the mastery of digital technology is the driving force behind the OFF, because our aim is also to discover the cinema of tomorrow. People who, to make a name for themselves, post videos on the Web, underground creations that we support through the Factory, in homage to Andy Warhol." As a result, the Great International Numeric Film Contest was born, and the winners are put in touch with professionals and receive support for the development of their projects.

On the program for these two evenings: " The Great Retrospective 2005-2013". The evening begins with a presentation of the artists, sponsors and jury members, followed by a cocktail reception with entertainment (fashion shows, musical show cases, painting and art exhibitions). Then it's the turn of the talents discovered internationally from 2005 to 2013 in the various categories to be presented, along with the members of the jury who, sensitized by their own experience, have supported this concept since 2005. All the winners will be on hand to talk about their development since being discovered by the OFF de Cannes.

The OFF retrospective will be chaired by Disney producer Max Howard, who will present the award for Best Director. 2013 patron Myriam Lamare (triple world boxing champion) will present the award for Best Actor.
Wednesday, May 22, presentation of the winners' works, speeches by jury members and screening of the film *Forbidden Visions* by Alain Zirah and Anne Gomis made with artists discovered by the OFF de Cannes: Bernard Destouches (No Limit, Mafiosa), Jovanka Sopalovic (Aubade, Visions Interdites), Francisco Brescia, Sean Connery lookalike and music by Fanny Leeb, Alan Reeves, Olivier Calmel, Boomin HM...
- Also scheduled he actor Sami Naceri (Taxi, Indigènes) sent a warm message of support to the OFF de Cannes team, which was read out on site.

Myriam LAMARE, OFF de Cannes godmother:

Myriam Lamare is the 2013 OFF de Cannes Godmother. Triple world boxing champion, WBA (2004-2006), WBF (2009-2011) and IBF (2011) by dominating Chevelle Hallback on points in Toulon, she has also been a PACA Regional Councillor since 2010. She took part in Koh-Lanta, le choc des héros until the semi-finals and lives in Marseille.

MAX HOWARD, Chairman of the Jury for the second year:

Max Howard: President of the Jury

Producer and actor, based in the USA for 23 years.. Former President of Warner Bros Feature Animation, he oversaw hits as *The Iron Giant* and *Space Jam*. At DreamWorks he co-produced the animated feature *Spirit, Stallion of the Cimarron*. Head of Max Howard Consulting, he is executive producer for Disney, he has set up films such as *Who Framed Roger Rabbit, The Little Mermaid, Beauty and the Beast* and *The Lion King*. He also set up the Disney studio in Paris and produced *Igor* as President of Exodus Film Group.

The members of the 2013 jury are:

Jay Schindell, graphic designer for Disney Studios on *The Lion King, Pocahontas, The Hunchback of Notre Dame, Hercules* and *Mulan*, joined George Lucas's ILM company, working on films such as *Star Wars Episode 2*, Steven Spielberg's *A.I.* and *Minority Report*, then, in Hollywood, on special effects for *Spiderman 2* and *3, I Robot, The Day After, The Return of Superman, Monster House* and many others. With Melwood Pictures, he has worked on films as varied as *The Spirit Bear* and *Iron Man 3*. Today, he's producing and directing his 1st feature, an animated science-fiction film, *Pastoral*, a romantic musical based on his own screenplay.

Laurie Gordon, Canadian film producer, lives in Montreal, where she is best known for producing Chris Landreth's 2005 Oscar-winning short film *Ryan*. Her company MusiVision, founded in 2004, has worked with several iconic animation directors, including Co Hoedeman, an award-winner, Ryan Larkin, an award-winner, and Gerald Potterton (The Beatles - The Yellow Submarine, Heavy Metal - Métal Hurlant), winner of three Academy Awards.

Petteri Pasanen is a Finnish producer of animated films, initially with Kinoproduction. In 2002, he created his own company, Anima Vitae, with which his first animated film *Niko, le petit renne* (2008) won a prize at the Cannes Film Festival with a gross 21M$ for more than 550,000 spectators for a budget of 6M$. By accident, he says. But he loves accidents of this kind. He just released the suite *Niko le petit renne 2* (2012) for more than 787,000 spectators in France.

Alan Reeves: This composer, producer and musician has a career studded with prestigious awards, including 35 Academy Awards. A brilliant pianist, he has accompanied such greats as: The Beatles, The Who, Prince, The Rolling Stones, The Animals, Rod Stewart, Chuck Berry, Lionel Ritchie, Gene Vincent, Serge Gainsbourg, Chaka Kahn, Manu Dibango, Otis Redding, Aznavour, Jimi Hendrix, Eric Clapton and many more. He has also composed the soundtrack for the Cannes Film Festival 2001 award-winning *To Walk with Lions, Ocean Oasis* for IMAX and Quentin Tarantino's *Kill Bill 2*.

Preity Üupala is an Australian actress, entrepreneur and philanthropist. Originally from the beautiful Bondi Beach in Sydney, Australia. She was discovered as an actress and beauty queen based in Los Angeles. Préity Üupala won worldwide acclaim as the recipient of three prestigious awards at the Asia Pacific Film Festival, held in December 2010, in China. After sharing the stage with actor Jackie Chan, she also gained more international fame, being crowned Miss India International AP 2012, in Los Angeles.

Afida Turner is an international singer, songwriter, actress most famous as TV host in France. The media call her The Tiger, which gives her a feeling of invincibility. Her challenge was to travel to the USA to learn the language. She then produced a second album, in English, to tackle the global market. In 2011, she opened a prime-time show on TF1 *Carré VIP* with a live performance of her new single *Come with me* and released her album *Paris-Hollywood* in May. She appears in her first French film: *Forbidden Visions and* promote her new song *Born an Angel*.

Paris-born supermodel **Feline Sabine** hails from the French West Indies. She took her first steps in fashion with a beauty contest where she won the title of Miss France Outremer. This was followed by a series of advertising, fashion and catwalk contracts that enabled her to gain experience and notoriety. She highlights her beloved Caribbean. The ambassador of Caribbean beauty, Feline Sabine represents the "Caribbean islands" so dear to her heart and will put her beauty at the disposal of cinema, at the world's most prestigious festival, as OFF de Cannes 2013 jury member.

PRESS CONFERENCE 2013

Tuesday May 21, 2013

The press conference was held in the bar of the Eden Hôtel, with the presentation to the media of the artists, sponsors, patrons and jury members. The various media appreciate the presence of Myriam Lamare, world boxing champion and godmother of the OFF de Cannes 2013. They then met Jay Schindell (SFX supervisor for Steven Spielberg and Iron Man 3), Alan Reeves (composer for Kill Bill 2), Laurie Gordon (Canadian producer of Animaze), Afida Turner (Franco-American singer), Petteri Pasanen (Prix du Jury 2018 Cannes festival), the Top Model Feline Sabine (Ambassadress of Carribean), Préity Üupala (Miss India), and made several interviews under the chairmanship of Max Howard (producer of The Lion King). The Carnet d'Art team, partners of Annecy OFF, was proud to interview Max Howard, who explained that during the Cannes Festival, everyone focuses on the red carpet. For him, the alternative is the OFF de Cannes, which presents artists who are often multidisciplinary and unclassifiable. The jury noted the quality of all the films selected by our Annecy OFF partners at this legendary event.

The press conference was followed by a nice cocktail reception before entertainment in the auditorium with fashion shows, musical show cases, contemporary lighting exhibition...

The ceremony - During the presentation of talents discovered at international level from 2005 to 2013 (already 8 years) in various categories, the members of the jury, sensitized by their own journey, were able to discover the show during which Alain Zirah and Anne Gomis presented the following artists to the public, with the support of Myriam Lamare, women's world boxing champion and godmother of the event:
- **Pin-Up Miss You, aka Shinta Delanoe,** actress and burlesque artist who performed two classy Jessica Rabbit striptease routines for the very attention of the producer of the film *Who Killed Roger Rabbit*?
- **Lyah**, a young singer revealed on the M6 TV show Popstars, who is preparing her first album.
- **Franck Katz**, painter and creator of *l'Art Subtil* (winner of the OFF de Cannes 2011) made a show with stylist Jelena Vujanovic (discovered at the OFF de Cannes 2012) and actress and singer Sandka Fée, all three of whom presented their painted garments in a mini fashion show in anticipation of the one to be held two days later, on May 23, at the Villa Oxygene.
- **Morgan Priest**, actor and film director (winner of the OFF de Cannes 2011) for his latest film *Predators* and a best of from his short films.
- **Richie River**, pianist and singer-songwriter, who will launch into a showcase and get the auditorium audience and jury members singing along.

The 2013 OFF de Cannes have taken the review of eight years of effort, work and conviction in bringing Arts to light. Alain Zirah and Anne Gomis are delighted to give a voice to the artists discovered by the team, who they believe, bring meaning to today's Art and will be part of the cultural scene's references in 2020. Benoit Comte from Annecy OFF complete the selection.

The films screening on May 21, 2013, are: **Predator** by Morgan Priest, praised by Max Howard (picture) **Love Gun Tatoo** by Guillaume Gomis and on May 22, 2013, **Famille Clown** by Jonathan Kahn, **Cry** by Yves Courbet, **Speed Rating** by Gil Kenel and Arnaud Raymackers as well as the Official Selection of films for Annecy OFF 2013:

P.I.O.K by Clément Dartigues and Théo Dusapin ECV Animations, *Since* by Cyril Algaro and Arnaud Laffond, **Krush** by Loïc Beslay and his team for ESRA Bretagne, **Dialogue between the deaf** by Sarah Lepreux, Anne Regnault and Marie Caroline Allard, **Cupidon** by Simon Bau and his team for ESMA 2013, D. N.A. 2.0 by François Bonnet ESRA 2013, **Get Wild** by Joseph Catté, Valentin Astier, Olivia Léonetti and Geoffrey Vattan - ArtFx 2012, **Milovan Circus** by Gerlando Infuso - la Cambre 2008, **Terraform** by Arthur Bayard and his team – ArtFx **Silent Trees** by Quentin Dubois and team.
Broken by Johann Troude, Johanna Olombel and Kevin Baudelle – ArtFx.

President Max Howard (The Lion King), Sabine Feline (Carribean Top Model), Alain Zirah (OFF de Cannes), Préity Üupala (Miss India), Jay Shindell (Iron Man 3), Petteri Pasanem (Anima Vitae) and the 35 awards Alan Reeves (Kill Bill 2) on The Eden stage for 2013 OFF de Cannes ceremony.

Alain Zirah, Joe Jackson, patriarch of the first musical family, Wes Madiko (Singer and musician from Cameroon), Simon Sahouri (president of The Jackson Family Foundation), for the Jackson Party in Villa Oxygene where they launch Michael Jackson credit card.

Simon Sahouri (president of The Jackson Family Foundation), Philippe Molin (Radio Prestige Cannes), Alain Zirah (Off de Cannes founder) during the 2013 Jackson party in Villa Oxygene.

Alain Zirah with Joe Jackson by the great deutch painter Klaus Jürgen Dobberke.

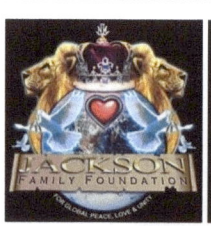

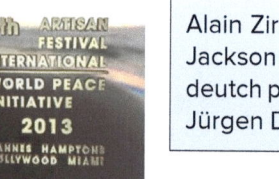

All the prize-winners spoke about their development since being discovered by the OFF de Cannes, presenting their latest news in a conference or on stage, and talking about the support they have received from professionals, jury members, media coverage and communication from the OFF de Cannes, thanks to which they were able to take flight. Jury members also shared their latest news.

On Wednesday, May 22, 2013, the presentation of the works of the winners, followed by the films of the partners (Annecy OFF, ART VIFF...), after the speeches of the members of the jury, was followed by the screening of the feature film *Forbidden Visions* by Alain Zirah and Anne Gomis, in the presence of the film crew, in the auditorium of the Eden Hôtel.

FORBIDDEN
VISIONS

The audience was then treated to the feature film *Forbidden Visions* by Alain Zirah and Anne Gomis, starring Afida Turner, Bernard Destouches, Jean-Luc Bosso, Jovanka Sopalovic, Nourry Falah, Alain Caporgno, Halidi M'Sa, Beatrice Touitou, Linda Cohen and many others...

Thanks to Jessica Miri, the *Forbidden Visions* crew was invited to attend the After-Party in the very private rooms of the Petit Carlton, on the Croisette.

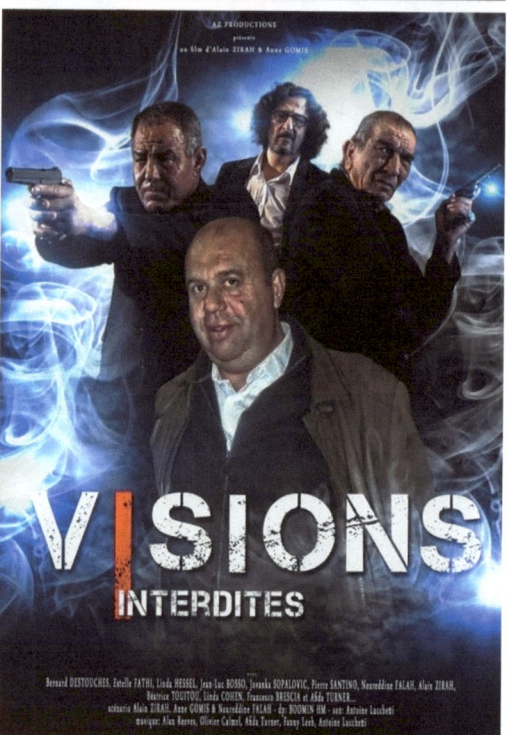

OFF DE CANNES 2013 WINNERS

May 2013 in Cannes.

The jury remarked on the quality of this very fine selection of films presented on May 21 and 22 at Eden Hotel, Cannes, with the partnership of Annecy OFF and Carnet D'art. Animated films were in the spotlight. And the winner is...

Best film: *Broken* by ARTFX collective **Johann Troude, Johanna Olombel** and **Kevin Baudelle.**

Best script and direction: *Speed Rating* by **Gil Kenel** and **Arnaud Raymackers.** Best universe and special effects: *Silent Trees* by **Quentin Dubois**.

Best music: **Gerlando Infuso** for the film *Milovan Circus,* La Cambre 2008.

Award certificates will be presented in Annecy on Friday, June 14, in a live TV show organized by partners ANNECY OFF and the set CARNET D'ART - Amistad prod in partnership with the OFF DE CANNES Festival.

Evening launch with **Benoit Comte, Patrick Mallet** TV8 Mont Blanc, Alain Zirah, Anne Gomis, Denis Vincenti, Frédéric Courant, Marie Tixier with screening of the film selection at the Annecy OFF Bar on the boat *Le Cygne.*

l'Essor Savoyard.fr

2013 06 20
Photo : Marie Jacquart

Après une édition réussie, le festival off veut continuer à prendre de l'ampleur

Pour sa troisième édition, le festival off a connu un joli succès. Cette année, le "off" avait été élu résidence sur le bateau "Le Cygne", grâce à un partenariat avec la Compagnie des bateaux.

Chaque jour, des films y ont été diffusés. Une centaine au total, de réalisateurs de moins de 25 ans et en provenance de nombreux pays dans le monde (Afrique, Etats-Unis, Europe), signe

que le "off" prend peu à peu sa place en marge du festival officiel.

Son co-fondateur, Thibaut Comte, se réjouit du bilan. « On a eu du monde tous les soirs, et surtout le vendredi qui a été une très grosse soirée. Je suis content de la semaine. Il y avait une ambiance conviviale et très simple. » Le président du "off" de Cannes avait notamment fait le déplacement.

L'an prochain, le Cygne de-

Thibaut Comte, Mehdi Meslem, Claire Martinod, avec le président du "off" de Cannes, Alain Zirah.

vrait de nouveau être mis à la disposition du festival off. Avec l'idée qu'un prix soit même décerné. Une catégorie vidéo devrait par ailleurs être créée afin d'étoffer l'événement. Bref, le "off" compte bien continuer son essor. « Ce que nous voulons, c'est que les Annéciens se sentent pleinement intégrés dans le festival off », souligne Thibaut Comte.

Dès le mois prochain, le site internet va être entièrement re-

fait et l'équipe va très rapidement plancher sur l'édition 2014 qui devrait être tout aussi excitante.

OLIVIER DURAND

TOUTE L'ÉQUIPE

L'organisation du festival off d'Annecy, c'est un groupe de six jeunes motivés : Mehdi Meslem, président, Thibaut Comte, directeur, Claire Martinod, Mélanie Chappaz, Théo Golfetto et Célia Ratto.

ANNECY ANIMATION FILM FESTIVAL

2013, June. During the Annecy Animation Film Festival, one of the world's most important festivals, Alain Zirah was proud to support his partners and the young founders of Annecy OFF for their third edition. Aboard the boat *Le Cygne*, the Carnet d'Art team organized a TV show each evening to welcome prestigious guests. A great synergy between talented partners. And **Marie Jacquart** as photographer.

Interviewed by **Antoine Guillot** for his TV show, Alain was happy to award the Grand Prix for Best Film and Best Special Effects to the 4'57" short film *Broken* by **Johann Troude, Johanna Olombel, Kevin Baudelle** (ArtFx 2012). A staggering, aesthetically pleasing voyage through space.

"Well done again for the Broken short we screened in Cannes on May 22 as part of the competition, and which won an award from the professional jury at the OFF de Cannes ceremony. The whole team is ready to follow you. We can't wait to see your next projects..."

OFF DE CANNES 2014

The website has become too heavy. The team therefore created a new website in 2013, much lighter and more fluid. previewed on the ARTE yacht by the journalist Eric Naulleau, Alain Zirah's new book, *Dieu a créé la Femme à son Image* (Editions Thierry Sajat 2014) was offered to some of the participants.

For the 67th edition of the festival, from May 14 to 25, 2014, the OFF de Cannes ceremony took place at the EDEN hotel under the presidency of Alan Reeves, 35 international Awards including the music for the film *Kill Bill 2*.

A press conference was held on May 17 at the Russian Pavilion, for ROSKINO TV's 90th birthday, with the participation of Stella Art International, Alain Zirah and Svoy Pocherk, the producer of the film *Rudolf Noureev, Rebellious Demon*, directed by Tatiana Malova which will be screened before the OFF de Cannes ceremony.

Photo : Stephane Doyen

The OFF de Cannes presented many of the artists at the EDEN Hotel & Spa Center. Screening of excerpts from the film Rudolf Noureev, Rebellious Demon. Then the battle Rudolf Noureev vs Michael Jackson, Performance art. Musical showcase by Dimitri Jackson Junior for *The Resurrection Of Michael Jackson*. Tribute to Nelson Mandela and the Dalai Lama in their action for Peace in the world and with the Doves for Peace by Franck Katz.

©Stéphane Doyen

The personalities featured this year are:
- **Alan Reeves**, 35 international awards including the soundtrack to the film *Kill Bill 2*. Born in England and living between Los Angeles and Berlin for over 30 years, he has played with The Beatles, The Rolling Stones, The Who, The Animals, Prince, David Gilmour, Eric Clapton, Rod Stewart, Yes, Otis Redding, Jimi Hendrix, Chuck Berry, Lionel Ritchie...
- **Michael Winkler** "The Glitterking" from Berlin
- **Franck Katz**, creator of the Doves for Peace.
- **Patrick Lachaud** La Locale TV presenter and ART FREEDOM exhibition coordinator.
- **Jessica Bijou Devillez**

©Stéphane Doyen

Once again, board members attended the Cannes Film Festival and other film festivals at their own expense. As in the previous year, some members of CINQ REGARDS were present at numerous events in Marseille and at a few festivals. The adventure continues

- in **Cannes,** with the film market;
- in **La Ciotat** for the Best of Short Films;
- in **Annecy** for the International Animation Film Festival and MIFA;
- in **Paris-Montparnasse** at Atelier Gustave for ART FREEDOM 2014).

The Chairman notes that AZ PRODUCTIONS has shot and produced short films and event teasers in Marseille, Annecy and Paris.

More information:

After lesoffdecannes.canalblog.com for the years 2005 to 2009, then 2010offdecannes.canalblog.com for 2010 and 2011, the association's various recent actions have been described on the new blog created by Alain Zirah: 2012offdecannes.canalblog.com.
The official website in 2010 was www.offdecannes.com

The new website created in 2013 was www.off-de-cannes.webs.com

Facebook : Les OFF de Cannes groupe officiel
Facebook : Le Grand concours International du Web
Facebook : Alain Zirah
Facebook : Anne Gomis

EDEN HÔTEL & SPA
★★★★
Cannes

Alain ZIRAH and Anne GOMIS

have the pleasure to invite you to attend
THE GREAT RETROSPECTIVE (2005-2015)

OFF DE *Cannes*

Since 2005, the OFF DE CANNES ceremony allows to discover and reward the talents of tomorrow, present in Cannes, during the Cannes festival.

Today, the New Talents express themselves with digital cameras and posts films on the web. They are the avant-garde of tomorrow International Cannes film festival that OFF DE CANNES completes with a new audience. The 2014 edition will put the limelight on ten years of efforts, work, or belief. Alain ZIRAH and Anne GOMIS will present some artists and personalities who, according to them, give a sense to the meaning of the Art and will be references in 2020.

Thursday, may 22, 2014 - EDEN HOTEL - 133 rue d'Antibes 06400 CANNES - FRANCE Free entry, mandatory registration on: alainzirah@yahoo.fr / formose@live.fr

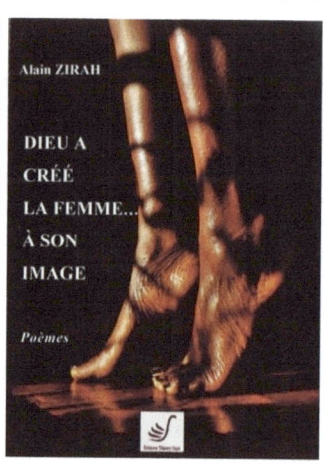

Alain ZIRAH

DIEU A
CRÉÉ
LA FEMME...
À SON
IMAGE

Poèmes

Rudolf
Nureyev
rebellious demon

Anne GOMIS, OFF de Cannes International Film Contest founder, will propose the Metamorphose of a woman as a princess. (Ph. A. Zirah)

Presentation of the e-book *CANNES FESTIVAL BACKSTAGE* and of the last book *GOD CREATED WOMAN ALIKE HERSELF* written by Alain ZIRAH (photo).

THE BATTLE NOUREEV vs JACKSON
The OFF de Cannes organise a Tribute to two dancers of exception: Rudolf NOUREEV and Michael JACKSON with a flash mob, May 17, and the resurrection live show with Dimitri Jackson Junior, May 22, in Eden Hôtel – Cannes after the screening of Rudolf Noureev rebellious demon by Tatiana MALOVA.

Thursday May 22, 2014 - EDEN HOTEL - 133 rue d'Antibes 06400 CANNES

19h - Press Conference with media presentation of some personalities, choosen to be the 2014 artists. The entire evening will be filmed by **BDM TV** broadcast's team who'll also conduct interviews for a TV program. Presentation of the ebook *Cannes Festival Backstage* and signature of the last book *God Created Woman ... Alike Herself.*

20H30 - OFF DE CANNES Ceremony in the auditorium.
Retrospective video What are OFF de Cannes - Presentation of the 2014 Artists.
Projection of a slideshow around Martial TAPOLO our 2014 fashion designer.

21H30 - Tribute to two dancers of exception: Rudolf NOUREEV and Michael JACKSON. Projection of the film *RUDOLF NOUREEV, THE REBEL DEMON* by Tatiana MALOVA product by SVOY POCHERK (Russia)

Rudolf **Nureyev** rebellious demon

Projection of the reportage on the Flash Mob with 50 fans of Michael Jackson on La Croisette, by Time is People who organized the Flash Mob in Paris for the promotion of the movie *This is it*. The Battle NOUREEV vs JACKSON has two winners fighting for the humanity...

Interviews followed by a cocktail with presentation of Fashion week artists to the medias, professionals from cinema, music and fashion, models and personalities.

22H30 - Showcase of Dimitri JACKSON Junior, 12.
Entry of the princess after the Metamorphosis and reactions of the audience and professionals.
23H - In the EDEN lounge, all the Michael Jackson's fans will sing the song for peace *We are the World*.

OFF DE CANNES 2015

MAKING WOMEN EVEN MORE BEAUTIFUL

AZ PRODUCTIONS & CONCEPT INITIATIVE PRESENT THE LAUNCHING OF THE GREAT INTERNATIONAL FILM CONTEST FOR OFF DE CANNES FROM JANUARY 2 TO APRIL 15.

Today, cinema has been complemented and even surpassed by television, computers and Smartphones...The talents of tomorrow are now expressing themselves with digital cameras and Smartphones to create original videos that they broadcast on the Internet. The web revolution is playing an essential role in the instant dissemination of images around the world.

Since 2011, Alain Zirah (AZ Productions) and Anne Gomis (Concept Initiative) have been organizing a competition to discover the "Talents of Tomorrow" in the categories of film, music, fashion and visual arts. This year, candidates are invited to express themselves and show what makes a woman even more beautiful (beauty, elegance, glamour, charm... everything that makes a woman feminine).

In a globalized world of political correctness, the candidates will be able to express their differences, think outside the box, indulge their fantasies with complete freedom of thought, and share their darkest and happiest ideas. "Les OFF de Cannes" will be rewarding web-based talent, destined to become future greats of the 21st century through their personal visions of women.

At the end of the competition, twenty-four candidates will be shortlisted at the OFF DE CANNES 2014 ceremony. They will then take part in the first WebTV show to culminate in the production of a film. Each week, one of them will leave the adventure, with the votes of the public. Eight finalists will direct the film together. AZ PRODUCTIONS will produce a film made by eight co-directors and musicians who don't know each other. Alain Zirah and the members of the jury will accompany them and give them advice on how to put together a feature-length film that will be premiered in Marseille, Paris and Cannes during the 2015 festival, for THE 10TH OFF DE CANNES ANNIVERSARY. A major media campaign will be launched throughout the year to publicize these artists, their work and the collective work that will be created.

The party was incredible and hot with the singer Stacey King with Anne Gomis in the Jackson party with Joseph Walter Jackson, patriarch of the first musical family.

After the Cannes Film Festival, as in the previous year, some members of the team were present at events in some festivals. Then Alain and Anne met up with Patrick Lachaud and Melissa Zigaut for the ART FREEDOM 2016 exhibition held at the Carrousel du Louvre, in Paris. The paintings of his mother Arlette Duran-Zirah received an Awards from Le Louvre for the quality of her knife-painting technique.

The OFF de Cannes took an active part in the World Peace Night at Richard Nilsson's Villa Oxygene, followed on May 23 by the closing ceremony at the Majestic for the Fashion Glam Couture Show.

Photo : Robert Martin

Photo : Dan Ngu

JAÏS NOTARI   MESSIKA CAMARA   LEA BERTONE

un film de
ALAIN ZIRAH

DANGEROUS LADIES

The World Peace Night at Villa Oxygene, with many stars, was followed by a special OFF de Cannes event with Red Carpet in La Ciotat, in the oldest theater ever where was born cinema.

Photos : Franz Fox Kennedy

Dangerous Ladies is a short film shot with entrance in Harley Davidson motorbike in an Indian restaurant and Girl Power as ever. The team meets up on the Cannes red carpet.

LA RENCONTRE

Tapis Rouge pour l'Eden avec les Off de Cannes !

Dimanche, strass et paillettes à l'Eden-Théâtre, où Alain Zirah, fondateur des Off de Cannes, a invité nombre d'artistes venus de Cannes, Avignon, Paris, Belgique…

Entre les vidéos du Off, plusieurs surprises, plongeant la salle pour quelques instants dans les coulisses de Cannes, avec pour invitée d'honneur Jessica Abandou, ambassadrice de la Jackson Family Foundation pour la Belgique, qui inaugura le tapis rouge avec sa belle traine de dentelle rose, les chanteurs John Maures et Tricia Mendy, la styliste Irène pour la marque Sise Ici avec un défilé-surprise de jolies robes en soie. On notait aussi la présence de Mister Provence et Miss Mormoiron, avec leur agent. Rencontre avec Alain Zirah.

▮ Pourquoi ce "Tapis rouge" ?

"Nous rentrons du festival de Cannes les yeux chargés d'images, et étant originaire de La Ciotat, je suis toujours déçu que le festival de cinéma ne se tienne pas là où a eu lieu la première projection au monde ! Ceci donc pour faire parta-ger l'univers du festival et ses paillettes aux Ciotadens. Et remettre en lumière les frères Lumière !

▮ Vous êtes engagé dans le cinéma ?

"Créateur des OFF de Cannes, je présente un documentaire sur les 10 ans de ce festival (2005-2015), un reportage réalisé par l'école IEJ de Pape Diouf et Jean-Pierre Foucault, avec la présence d'invités de retour du festival de Cannes 2015. Et Anne Gomis est la créatrice du Grand Concours du Film Numérique sur le Web, qui permet à des artistes du monde entier de présenter leurs films de 3'. On espère y voir un jour des Ciotadens primés !"

▮ Quels sont vos projets ?

"J'ai côtoyé en dix ans de Off 3700 artistes, mon souhait est de revenir chaque année dérouler le Tapis rouge pour attirer ici les cinéastes du monde entier, dans la ville où ont été tournés les premiers films, et où se trouve le premier cinéma au monde !"

Ch.H.

▮ Strass et paillettes à l'Eden-théâtre, où Alain Zirah, fondateur des Off de Cannes, invitaient ses amis artistes. / PHOTO C.H.

OFF DE CANNES 2016

For the 69th edition of the festival, from 2016, May 11 to 22, a press conference was held on May 13 at Rado Plage, on the Croisette, with the participation of Serena Zouaghi, Hugo Mayer, the Sarasvati screenwriters' collective. The OFF de Cannes showcased many of the artists in Cannes, during the beautiful Tiffany Red Carpet event in the Grand Salon du Carlton on May 17.

The final of the OFF de Cannes Grand Concours International du Web was held during the GSF Awards gala dinner in the Grand Salon du Carlton on Saturday, 2017, May 20, with Anne Gomis, Alain Zirah, Andres Aquino, Dr. Antonio Gellini, Carolien der Linden, Stavroulla Nicolaou...

The Great International Web Contest marks its comeback.

Alain Zirah's new book, Blood on Red Carpet (Editions Thierry Sajat 2016) marks the first volume in the adventures of the Kat Ladies, who have often been in the spotlight at Cannes' OFF. The book was previewed at the Carrousel du Louvre, where it was awarded the Prix Art Freedom 2016 during the FIAC! week (Foire Internationale d'Art Contemporain).

This year's featured personalities are **Michael Errington**, a French-English pianist and film composer living in Berlin (Unconditional Love, The Flood, The Lost World of the Crystal Skull). He has made a name for himself playing for Brad Pitt and Angelina Jolie, and last year for Leonardo Di Caprio's The Heart Funds. As a gesture of friendship to the Cannes OFFs, he performed the piano rendition of the piece he played for the Brangelina couple (Brad Pitt & Angelina Jolie) at Château de Miraval.

Movin' Melvin Brown, soul singer and tap dancer, accompanied by Francesca Sansalone.
The New York singer **Judi Beecher**.

Yves Bordes and Alain Zirah, whose three-part photo call features a visual of Kat Ladies: The origins, skillfully drawn by illustrator Yves Bordes. The photo call will be displayed in the grand salon of the Intercontinental Carlton on the GSF Awards/OFF gala evening in Cannes. It will also be displayed in the grand salon of the Majestic for the Fashion Glam Couture Show.

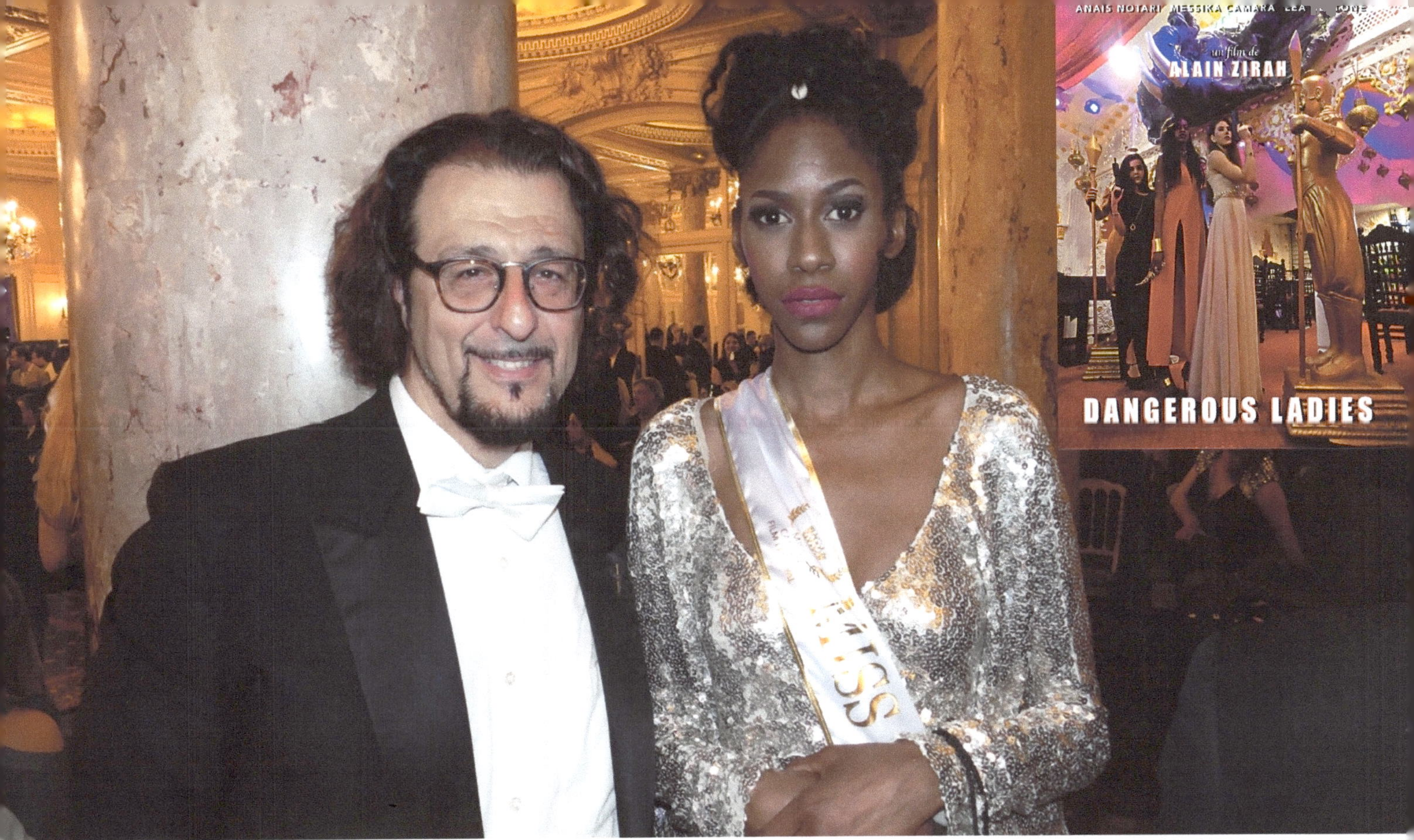

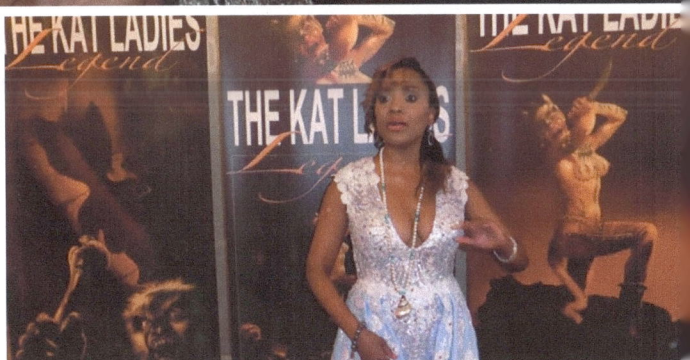

ALAIN ZIRAH
DANGEROUS LADIES

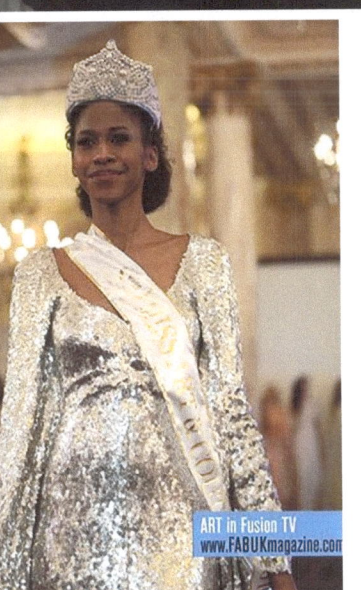

ART in Fusion TV
www.FABUKmagazine.com

Alain is very proud to see *Dangerous Ladies (2015)* lead Messika Camara awarded a beauty prize at the Carlton. The partner Tiffany McCall highlights *The Kat Ladies Legend* by Yves Bordes.

THE KAT LADIES
Legend

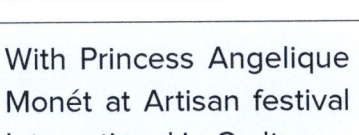

With Princess Angelique Monét at Artisan festival International in Carlton...

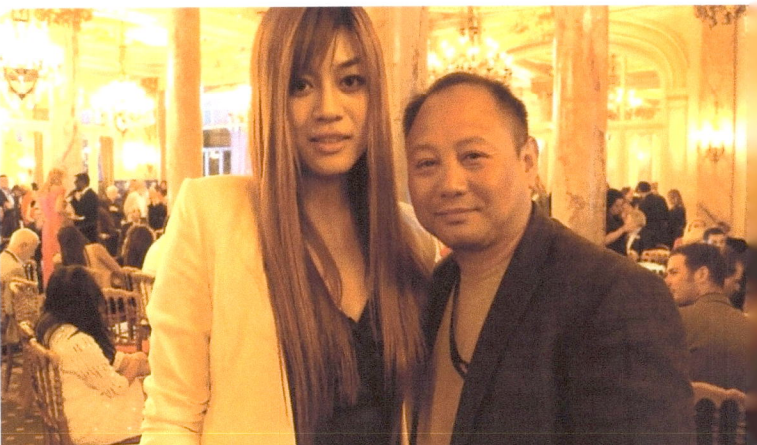

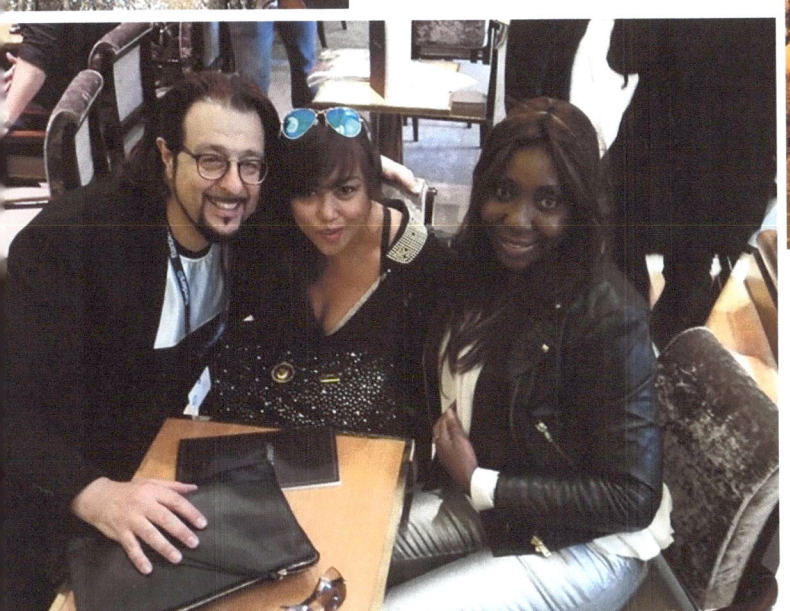

The ever-present friendship with **Angelique Brando** and the Tibetan rebel monk and writer **Tenzin Kunchap**.

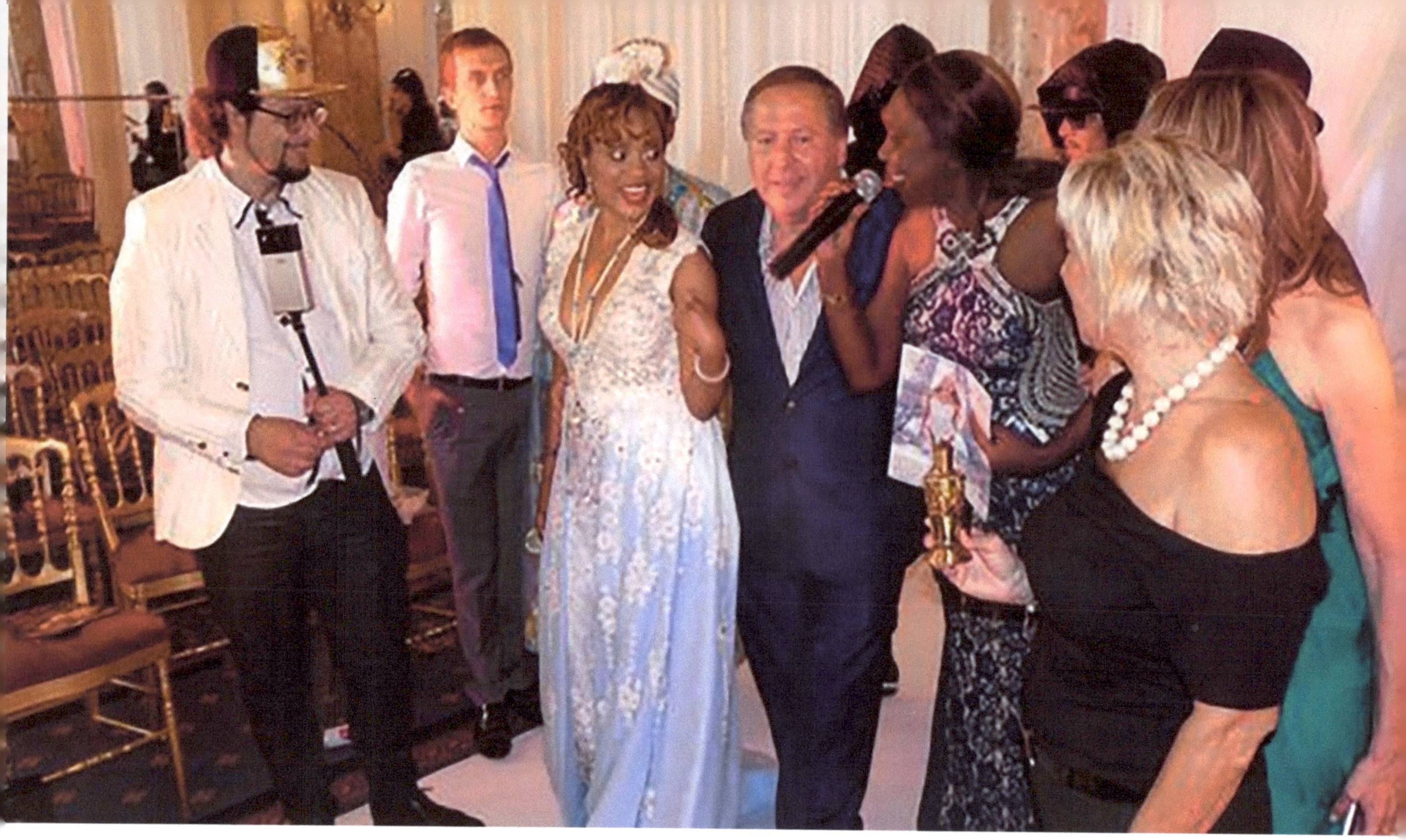

MENU

LUXE.TV

You Tube 4K
New !

Dailymotion 4K
New !

Français

FIND OUT HOW YOU CAN RECEIVE LUXE.TV
(Click here)

A 7-minute spot was shown on a loop on Luxe TV.

RETURN

FASHION SHOW: TIFFANY'S RED CARPET WEEK CANNES

France

OFF DE CANNES 2017

GREAT INTERNATIONAL WEB CONTEST: THE DREAM

Yesterday, great directors started out with short films. Today, new talents are expressing themselves with increasingly sophisticated Smartphones, and they're broadcasting their videos all over the world, thanks to the web revolution. This is the theme of the Grand Concours International du Web. The Cannes OFF ceremony was held on Saturday, May 20, 2017, during the GSF Awards gala dinner in the Grand Salon du Carlton, with Anne Gomis, Alain Zirah, Andres Aquino, Dr. Antonio Gellini, Carolien Ter Linden, Stavroulla Nicolaou and Justin Wallner.

The producers and Dr Antonio Gellini were delighted to announce the winners of the Grand Concours International du Web.

Music category: The nominees are Eddie Deschamps aka Eddie Diese (France), Mohombi (Congo). And the Winner is... **Mohombi** (Congo).

Plastic Arts category: The nominees are Werner Schulist (Germany), Steven Neill (Canada), Mariam Lamrani (Switzerland)
Favorite: **Mariam Lamrani aka May-Panda** (Switzerland). And the Winner is... **Werner Schulist** (Germany).
Category Films: The nominees are Pascal Lastrajoli (France), Yann Lerat (France), Alioune Sane (Senegal).

Favorite: **Alioune Sane** (Senegal). And the Winner is... **Pascal Lastrajoli** (France).

Fashion category: The nominees are Sabine Felyne (Caribbean), Carolien ter Linden (Holland), Sanjay Ramcharam (Holland).
Two favorites ex-aequo: **Sabine Felyne** (Caribbean) & **Sanjay Ramcharam** (Holland). And the Winner is... **Carolien ter Linden** (Holland).

Categorie Blog: The nominees are G-Laurentine (Cameroon), Zlata Devic Salaj (Croatia), Anik Couble (France).
Favorite: **Zlata Devic Salaj** (Croatia). And the winner is... **Anik Couble** (France).

Categorie Casting: The nominees are Philamanda Pro, Maria Sanchez (Spain) & Kary Ima (France).
Favorite: Philamanda Pro... And the Winners are... **Maria Sanchez** (Spain) & **Kary Ima** (France) ex-aequo.

Beauty Contest category organized by our partner Stavroulla Nicolaou for Prestige Show Production.
Coup de coeur: **Anastasia Terzi** (Greece) becomes Miss Greece 2017. And the winner is... **Nera Lesic** (Croatia) who became Miss Europe World 2017 and will compete in the Miss Universe contest.

LAUNCHING OF ALAIN ZIRAH'S BOOKS IN CARLTON
OFF DE CANNES/GSF AWARDS GALA – SATURDAY MAY 20, 2017

L'Intercontinental Carlton Cannes son grand salon et ses artistes prestigieux.

Anne Gomis

L'auteur Alain Zirah

Dr Antonio Gellini (Paramount) n

Igor Bogdanov

Sur scène avec les Bodyguards Nyl-R

After Anne Gomis performance of her song Feel Good, in Carlton, the winners of the contest took part in the shooting of Kat Ladies digital series produced by AZ Productions (Alain Zirah) and Angie'Films (Angelica Rutigliano).

The winners Maria Sanchez, Nera Lesic, Anastasia Terzi and Carolien ter Linden were honored as lead actresses in the 1st episode (pilot) of the *Kat Ladies* series, May 23 to 26 on the Croisette, in prestigious private parties of the 70th Cannes festival, including Richard Nilsson's World Peace Night at Villa Oxygen, Super Cannes, and GSF Awards Gala with Andres Aquino. The Dr Olympia Gellini endorses Alain and Anne for Family Film Awards organization.

SPECIAL WEB

KAT LADIES

OFF
de
CANNES
RETROSPECTIVE

OFF DE CANNES retrospective 2005 - 2020

Since 2005, the OFF de Cannes have been discovering avant-garde talent. In 15 years, Alain Zirah and Anne Gomis have put in limelight over 8,000 artists in film, music, fashion, writing and the Visual arts, and organized Joseph Jackson's first visit to Cannes.

Équipe OFF de CANNES

The Great International Web Contest completes the line-up each year, with a jury of professionals including Max Howard (The Lion King), Jay Shindell (Iron Man 3), Emir Kusturica (2 Palmes d'Or), Jan Kounen (Blueberry), Alan Reeves (Kill Bill 2), Olympia Gellini (Family Films Awards), Steven Nia (Avengers Endgame). **WWW.OFF-DE-CANNES.WEBS.COM**

Filming of the Kat Ladies web series by Alain Zirah during the 70th Cannes Film Festival 2017.

"WE DON'T MAKE EVENTS, WE WRITE A LEGEND."

2019 Masterclass cinema at Majestic.

2019 Carlton & diner with the Women Leaders at Fouquet's.

2019 photo shooting before Magnificent party at villa Jolie on 3 levels.

2019 Bar des Célébrités of Carlton with patron Paul Loup Sulitzer.

2018 Carlton ballroom, Bivouac, World Peace Night at villa Oxygene.

2017 the Carlton ballroom, Family Film Awards, GSF, yacht, World Peace Night.

2016 the Carlton ballroom, the Rado Beach, World Peace Night, Fashion Glam at Majestic

2015 Cannes Fashion Week and Fashion Festival at Majestic.

2014 Grand Hotel and finale in the Eden Hotel Auditorium

2013 screening of the film Forbidden Visions and OFF de Cannes ceremony at the Eden Hotel

2013 OFF de Cannes ceremony at Eden Hotel with The Lion King, Iron Man 3 and Kill Bill 2 and Villa Oxygene

2012 Atrium Beach, screening at Les Arcades Theater and ceremony on Carlton Beach

2011 Hotel Embassy, Jackson Family press conference and Awards ceremony at Villa Oxygene

2010 Le Carré d'Or then spectacular ceremony at the Petit Bar du Carlton

2009 ANBTV television ceremony on Majestic Barrière pontoon.

2008 Hotel 3.14 Rooftop with Group Partouche sponsorship.

2007 Salon Palme d'or at Martinez with Emir Kusturica in the chair.

2005 Creation OFF de Cannes ceremony in the Lounge of the Majestic Barrière.

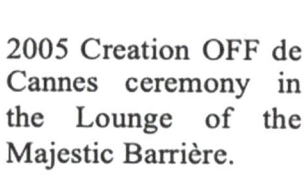

PRESS REVIEW

225

MEDIAS PARTNERS

They broadcast us

ALAIN ZIRAH

A multi-talented artist, Alain Zirah, writer, photographer and director, is Total Art founder. He created the OFF de Cannes in 2005, which he has co-produced with Anne Gomis in prestigious venues since 2011. He received the Who's Who Worldwide Awards (Los Angeles), in 2015. Since 2016, Alain and Anne co-produce the Family Film Awards with Olympia A. Gellini. They become members of the World Film Institute in 2021. They are preparing the 20th anniversary of the OFF de Cannes festival for May 2025.

As specialist of the Cannes festival, where he has been visiting since 1983, Alain has published several books and the novel *Blood on the Red Carpet* (Prize Art Freedom 2016). His autobiographies *Glitter & Glam* (2011) and *Cannes festival Backstage* (2017) were completed with the biography of Alain Zirah and Anne Gomis in *Cannes Backstage* (2023).

With Nicolas Biolley, Alain directed the feature *The Kat Ladies* (2009), and, with Anne Gomis, the feature film *Forbidden Visions* (2013) presented during the Cannes Film Festival. He shot movies about the Girl Power as *Power Pop Girls* (2019) and the series *Kat Ladies* produced by Angie Films and AZ Productions. With Anne Gomis, he presented 4 shows called *20/20 Culture* for his YouTube Channel, before they made some International WebTV shows with Blackfeeling.

As photographer since 1983, for the Imapress agency and president of the Maisons-Laffitte photo-club, he received an Award in Paris for his 30-years career in fashion and celebrity photography, from his first exhibition *The Flowers of Male Evil* (Marseille 1983). With Art Freedom, he participates in exhibitions at Atelier Gustave (2014), Espace Pierre Cardin (Paris 2015) and Business Art at the Carrousel du Louvre (Paris 2016).

His universe of Girl Power appears in his books *God created Woman* (2014) and *Forbidden to Men* (Prix Cap sur le Monde 2019), and he published his first American book *God created Woman alike herself* (2023). The Prize of Castellet 2022 and 2023 are awarded for his literary work as a whole (2022) and for *God created Woman Alike Herself* with an Awards from Lithe-Litho Le Castellet 2023.

As a Avant-garde digital artist, he received two World of Winners Awards, (London), including Best Artist 2020 and the Superstar Awards for Best NFT from Superstar-Art Foundation, (Dallas), during the Cannes Festival 2023.

Photo : Remy Barral

ANNE GOMIS

OFF de Cannes Festival co-producer with Alain Zirah, since 2011, she founded The Great International Web Contest to expend the event into international. Anne is also Vice-President of Cinq Regards.

Native from a Guinea Bissau family, born in Dakar, Senegal, she arrived in France when she was 4 and only spoke in wolof. Later she learned that she is a real Princess Adji Biagui of two villages in Casamance, as like her cousin the international American artist Whoopi Goldberg, born Biagui. She organized *Miss Black beauty queen* and celebrate *Miss Night*. As manager of The B52, the first French rappers' nightclub for 7 years, she discovered IAM who became the most famous South of French Rap band and get a label for their first record and the first part of Madonna shows in Paris.

In the event business since the age of 19, she rented venues and organized parties under different themes in the South of France. Forerunner for Miss Black France, promotion of Djo Balard (the King of the Black Mic Mac sapping), Miss Night (contest of 17 nightclubs closed for the occasion and gathered in the discotheque La Plage). Afterwards, she was manager for 7 years of a nightclub in front of the Opera de Marseilles: *B52* and then *The Appart.* In 2021, she organized with Alain Zirah the Garden Party of July 14th, during Cannes festival and one week with Djo Balard at the OFF de Cannes Pool Party, at the end of summer.

With the expansion of her work, she was requested by several personalities for collaborations as like Max Howard (Pocahontas, Lion King), Jay Schindell (Iron Man 3) and was applied by the Jackson Family Foundation to become a part of the press conference during the first coming in Cannes festival, France, of the King of Pop Michael Jackson's father, Joseph Jackson.

Co-producer and Agent for the OFF de Cannes' Factory during the Cannes Film Festival, since 2011, she co-directed with Alain Zirah the feature film *Forbidden Visions/Visions Interdites*, in 2013. Anne Gomis is also co-producer of the Family Films Awards since 2016 she has been co-producer of the Family Films Awards since 2016 with Dr Olympia A. Gellini. Then became co-producer and member of the World Film Institute, in 2021.

Photo : Fox Eye

www.ingramcontent.com/pod-product-compliance
Lightning Source LLC
Chambersburg PA
CBHW041425120626
46547CB00002B/106